S0-CFF-216

FUNDED BY
GOALS 2000
A GRANT AWARDED
BY THE MICHIGAN STATE
DEPARTMENT OF EDUCATION.

SOJOURNER TRUTH

Peter Krass

MELROSE SQUARE PUBLISHING COMPANY
LOS ANGELES, CALIFORNIA

MELROSE SQUARE PUBLISHING COMPANY
LOS ANGELES, CALIFORNIA

Senior Consulting Editor for Chelsea House
Nathan Irvin Huggins
Director
W.E.B. Du Bois Institute for Afro-American Research
Harvard University

Consulting Editors for Melrose Square
Raymond Friday Locke
Antony Stately

Cover Painting: Jesse J. Santos
Cover Design: Jeff Renfro

SOJOURNER TRUTH

MELROSE SQUARE BLACK AMERICAN SERIES

ELLA FITZGERALD
singer

NAT TURNER
slave revolt leader

PAUL ROBESON
singer and actor

JACKIE ROBINSON
baseball great

LOUIS ARMSTRONG
musician

SCOTT JOPLIN
composer

MATTHEW HENSON
explorer

MALCOLM X
militant black leader

CHESTER HIMES
author

SOJOURNER TRUTH
antislavery activist

CONTENTS

1

"Aren't I a Woman?"   9

2

A Child of Darkness   23

3

Out of Bondage   41

4

A True Believer   65

5

God's Pilgrim   87

6

Calling Cards   109

7

A House Divided   131

8

"I Want to Ride!"   151

Chapter One

"Aren't I A Woman?"

ONE BRIGHT MORNING in 1852, hundreds of well-dressed men and women gathered in a church in Akron, Ohio, for the opening session of an annual convention on women's rights. Although the building was usually reserved for prayer, during the next few days it was to serve as a meetinghouse where people could discuss whether women deserved to have the same political and social rights as men. Some of the conventioneers had come from hundreds of miles away to talk about this burning issue.

The men and women greeted one another,

As a traveling lecturer, Truth used her powerful speaking manner and keen wit to win support for the women's rights and antislavery movements.

then took their seats in the church and eagerly waited for the opening session to convene. As they were waiting, their attention was drawn to a woman who stood gazing at them from the back of the church. All of the conventioneers were white; this woman was black, however, and she presented a striking figure. She stood more than six feet tall and wore a plain gray dress, metal-rimmed eyeglasses, and an oversized sunbonnet. She was more than 50 years old.

Seeing that there were no empty seats at the back of the church, the black woman walked slowly down an aisle to the front, holding her head high in a proud, almost defiant manner. When she reached the front pews, she did not sit down with the others. Instead, she sat alone, on one of the steps leading up to the pulpit.

Many of the conventioneers craned their necks to get a better look at this lone figure. They tried to guess her identity and her purpose in attending the meeting. "An abolition affair!" said one man, guessing that the woman was a traveling lecturer who made speeches against slavery. During the first half of the 19th century, a powerful antislavery movement had begun in the United States, with abolitionist leaders such as William Lloyd

In May 1852, Truth made a stirring speech in support of equality for women at the second annual women's rights convention in Akron, Ohio. The title page of the record of the previous year's meeting is shown here.

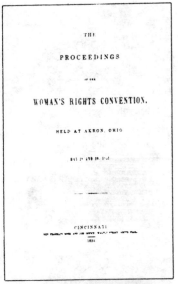

THE

PROCEEDINGS

OF THE

WOMAN'S RIGHTS CONVENTION,

HELD AT AKRON, OHIO

CINCINNATI

1851

Garrison and Frederick Douglass becoming known throughout the North as they traveled from town to town, speaking against the injustices of slavery.

Everyone's attention was eventually diverted away from this woman when Frances Gage, who was presiding over the convention, stood to introduce the morning's first speaker. After the opening speech had been made, other speakers came to the lectern. Because anyone who wished to speak could do so at a women's rights meeting, some of the people who came to the lectern supported the women's movement, while others spoke against it.

An abolitionist leader and outstanding orator, Frederick Douglass attended many women's rights conferences and was a strong advocate of feminist causes. The masthead of his antislavery newspaper, the North Star, *featured the motto "Right is of no sex—Truth is of no color."*

As the speakers came and went, the woman in the sunbonnet remained on the pulpit steps, sitting in such a way that her face was sunk into the hollow of her hands. But even though she sat in this seemingly self-absorbed manner, she was paying attention to what was being said.

At the conclusion of the morning session, Gage called for a midday intermission, the black woman walked among the conventioneers, offering to sell them copies of her book, entitled *The Narrative of Sojourner Truth.* Although she could not read or write, the woman had produced an account of her life by dictating her personal history to a friend.

The resulting book told of Sojourner Truth's life as a slave, of her liberation from slavery, and of how she was committed to helping other slaves gain their freedom. This commitment was so great that she had become one of the most articulate and outspoken antislavery activists in the country. She soon became one of the leading women's right activists as well.

Like many of the women who had become involved in the movement to free blacks from slavery, Truth came to realize that women in America needed to be liberated, too. They were not allowed to vote and had few opportunities to gain a higher education or work in

At the Akron convention, chairperson Frances Gage rejected the pleas of those who asked her to prevent Truth from speaking at the meeting.

a profession. When Elizabeth Cady Stanton, Lucretia Mott, and the other pioneers of women's rights began to lobby for women's rights in the late 1840s, Truth was ready to join their fight.

At first, many of the abolitionists worked with the women's rights groups. But when the nationwide debate over the abolition of slavery grew more heated, some supporters of the women's rights movement began to call for a separation of the two groups. They feared that their association with the abolitionists would imperil their crusade for women's rights, for although the issue of whether women were entitled to the same rights as men was certainly controversial, the practice of slavery was a topic that sometimes provoked dramatic—and often deadly—action.

When some of these separatists saw Truth at the women's rights convention in Akron, they became determined not to let her speak. During the midday break, several of them gathered around Gage and asked her to prevent Truth from addressing the convention later that afternoon. "It will ruin us," said one man, who claimed that the newspaper would then describe the conventioneers as a bunch of abolitionist agitators. But Gage refused to make any promises. "We shall see when the time comes" was all that she would say.

Yet Truth did not rise to speak during the afternoon session; she sat in the shadow of the pulpit steps and remained silent. During the morning of the convention's second day, she again appeared to be content merely to listen to the speakers (most of whom were men, for few people in the 19th century thought that it was proper for a woman to give an address in public). Among those who spoke were

Men frequently commanded the podium at early women's rights meetings until feminist leaders such as Susan B. Anthony, Elizabeth Cady Stanton, and Lucretia Mott helped to overturn the social convention that women not give public addresses.

several clergymen.

The first minister who stood before the conventioneers told them that men were entitled to "superior rights and privileges" because they possessed superior intelligence when compared with women. The next minister defended the domination of women by men on the grounds that Jesus Christ had been a man. "If God had desired the equality of women," the minister said, "He would have given some token of His will through the birth, life, and death of the Savior."

Another minister said that women had a lower status than men because of the original sin committed by Eve in the Garden of Eden. Yet another minister explained that the inherent inferiority of women was proven by their need to have men hold doors open for them. He said that women did not deserve the same rights as men because they were so much weaker.

All of these ministers believed that their sermons, championing the superiority of men, had dispelled the audience's enthusiasm for women's rights. In fact, the views of these ministers had proven to be extremely upsetting to many of the women in the audience. Yet none of the women seemed prepared to argue in public with such well-respected clergymen.

Then Truth arose and walked up to the lectern. "Don't let her speak!" cried a half-dozen men sitting near Gage. Truth removed her sunbonnet, and then she turned toward Gage, seeking permission to speak freely. Gage hesitated for a moment, then stood and introduced Truth to the audience.

"Well, children," Truth began in a low, soft voice. She was determined to rebut the ministers who had used Jesus and the Bible

Lucretia Mott (center) and another feminist are escorted from a lecture hall by an angry group of men who have broken up a women's rights meeting. During her lecture tours, Truth was subjected to similar hostilities.

to argue against women's rights. Even though she could not read, she knew every word printed in the Bible, and she was certain that none of them said that women were less than men any more than they said that blacks should be slaves.

"Where there is so much racket," Truth continued, "there must be something out of kilter." That "something," she added, was the domination of women and blacks by white men. The supporters of this unequal order "will be in a fix pretty soon," she said, thanks to the efforts of abolitionists and feminists.

Truth then turned to the minister who had said that women were too weak to deserve equal rights. How could that be? she asked. Nobody had ever helped her into a carriage, or ever carried her over a mud puddle, or ever given her the best place anywhere. She paused for effect and pulled herself upright so that her tall frame was even more imposing than usual.

Then, in a loud voice which sounded to some in the audience like rolling thunder, Truth said, "And aren't I a woman? Look at me! Look at my arm!" She rolled up a sleeve of her dress all the way to the shoulder and held out her arm. It was not a plump arm—the kind that most women saw in their mirrors each morning when they got dressed. Her arm, after many years of hard labor, was lean and sinewy.

"I have plowed, and planted, and gathered into barns, and no man could head me," Truth said. "And aren't I a woman?" She declared that she had worked as hard as any man—and that she could eat as much as a man, too, although many times she had gone hungry. She had borne children, only to watch them sold into slavery. When she missed them and cried, she said, no one but Jesus heard her sobs.

Truth next turned to the minister who had

argued that women were less intelligent than men and therefore did not deserve equal rights. What did intelligence have to do with rights? she wanted to know. Then she chastised the minister by pointing a finger at him and giving him an angry stare.

Next came the minister who had stated that women must be inferior because God had made Jesus a man. "Where did your Christ come from?" Truth asked the question again and then answered herself: "From God and a woman. Man had nothing to do with Him."

Finally, Truth confronted the minister who had spoken of Eve and the original sin. Once again she gave an impressive defense of women, telling the conventineers, "If the first woman God ever made was strong enough to turn the world upside down, all alone, these together"—and with this she glanced at the women in the audience—"ought to be able to turn it back and get it right side up again." This comment, which resulted in applause from most of the audience, was followed by her statement "Now old Sojourner hasn't got nothing more to say."

Many of the men and women in the audience immediately left their seats to congratualte Truth, and she in turn thanked them for their support. The path that she was following, from

Truth worked hard to obtain equal rights for all men and women, no matter how poor and uneducated they might be. Attacking the then widely held belief that women were less intelligent than men, she said, "Suppose a man's mind holds a quart, and a woman's don't hold but a pint; if her pint is full, it's as good as his quart."

the darkness of slavery to the daylight of freedom, was long and hard, and so she greatly appreciated any encrouragement that she received along the way—especially since a difficult stretch of road still lay ahead. Her greatest hope was that this road would ultimately lead to a place where all men and women were free and equal. But until she arrived there, she had little time to rest. It still seemed so far away.

Chapter Two

A
Child of
Darkness

SOJOURNER TRUTH WAS born into slavery in Hurley, New York, in around 1797. (As happened with many slaves, her master, a farmer of Dutch descent named Johannes Hardenbergh, did not record her exact date of birth.) Her parents were slaves named Betsey and James who lived on a farm near the Hudson River in upstate New York. They originally named their ninth child Isabella, but she changed her name to Sojourner Truth when she was about 46 years old.

Isabella's parents were overjoyed by the birth of their new child, but they were also

Born about 1797 as the ninth child of a slave couple in upstate New York, Truth was named Isabella at birth. Until her early thirties, she lived near towns such as this one on the Hudson River.

A slave waits to be sold at an auction in New Netherlands, the Dutch colony that in 1664 was conquered by the British and renamed New York. Slaves were a significant part of the economy there until well into the 1800s.

afraid for her. Their other sons and daughters had all been sold to other masters, and Betsey and James knew that the same fate might befall Isabella.

At that time, slaves had been bought and sold in the New York area for more than 150 years. In 1626, Dutch settlers in a colony named New Netherlands began importing blacks from Africa to work on their farms. Thirty-eight years later, the British seized the colony, renamed it New York, and brought in many more slaves. By 1723, blacks made up 15 percent of New York's population. Although slaves were not nearly as common in the northern colonies as they were in the southern colonies, they were still an important part of the economy.

When the Dutch lost possession of New Netherlands, many of the settlers remained in the colony and became British subjects. And when the American colonies declared their independence from Great Britain in 1776, many of them became U.S. citizens. Nonetheless, many of the Dutch Americans—including Hardenbergh—clung to their native language, and so Isabella was taught to speak Dutch rather than English while she was growing up.

When Isabella was about three years old, Hardenbergh died, leaving her, her parents, and 10 other slaves to his son, Charles. Having recently built a large limestone house in the nearby hills, Charles Hardenbergh moved these inherited slaves to the building's cellar. In this one dank and filthy room, Isabella and the other slaves ate and slept.

During the day, only a small amount of light shone through the cellar's small window. At night, the slaves lit the room with a fire and rested on hard wooden pallets. When it rained, water seeped through cracks in the walls and turned the floor into a pool of mud. Dur-

ing winter, the slaves sought to fight off the cold by wrapping themselves in worn blankets.

Despite being mistreated by Hardenbergh, who forced his slaves to endure such harsh living conditions, Isabella's parents remained obedient to him and worked hard at plowing and harvesting the crops in his fields. Conse-

A line of chained slaves is driven to a market in the Deep South. Although slaves in the northern states were generally treated better than those living in the South, they nonetheless were subjected to harsh working conditions and had few legal rights.

quently, their master developed some affection for the couple and eventually gave them a plot of land so that they could grow their own corn, tobacco, and other crops to trade with neighbors for additional food and clothing.

Soon after Isabella and her parents moved to Hardenbergh's farm, her brother Peter was

born. One night, when both children were still very young, their mother took them outside and told them to sit under a tree.

"My children," she said to them, "there is a God who hears and sees you."

The children asked her where God lived.

"He lives in the sky," their mother answered, "and when you are beaten, or cruelly treated, or fall into any trouble, you must ask help of him, and he will always hear and help you." She promised them that they were under

Truth spent her first 11 years on a farm near the town of Hurley, New York. The main street of the town is shown here as it appeared in the late 19th century.

God's protection.

Convinced that she was being looked after by a powerful guardian in the sky, Isabella faced difficulties in her life with increased confidence. Her self-confidence continued to grow as she got older and learned how to do new things. On Sundays, when she and the other slaves did not have to work their master's fields and orchards, she learned how to row a boat and ride a horse. She also learned from her mother to obey her master, to recite the

Slaves who worked on New York farms were responsible for a variety of chores. In addition to plowing fields and harvesting wheat, corn, and other crops, they also fished and hunted.

Lord's Prayer each day, and never to steal or lie.

However, Isabella also had other, darker lessons to learn. One night, when she heard her mother crying, she asked her what was wrong. Her mother replied, "I'm groaning to think of my poor children. They don't know

where I be, and I don't know where they be. They look up at the stars, and I look up at the stars, but I can't tell where they be."

Isabella later heard of the manner in which her older brother Michael and older sister Nancy had been taken away from their family many years before. On a snowy winter morn-

The cabins in which slaves lived were often drafty, windowless buildings. At night, workers gathered around the fireplace not only to warm themselves but to share news and tell stories.

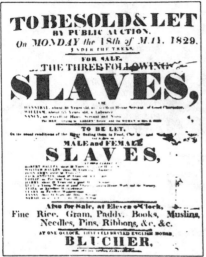

Perhaps the most heartrending experience that slaves had to endure was to see their families divided up at a public auction. Elderly slaves who were no longer able to work were sometimes freed and left to fend for themselves.

ing, some men in a horsedrawn sled had stopped at the cabin where Isabella's family then lived. Michael was delighted when the men told him that he was going for a ride and quickly jumped aboard the sled. The boy became frightened, however, when one of the men walked out of the cabin carrying a large box that contained his sister Nancy. She was screaming.

Suddenly growing scared, Michael leapt off the sled, ran inside the cabin, and hid under a bed. But the men dragged him out, put him on board the sled, and drove away. Isabella's parents, who had been helpless to protect their family from the slave traders to whom their master had sold the children, never saw Michael or his sister again.

Despite her parents' fears that Isabella, too, would be sold at an early age, the family remained intact until Isabella was about 11 years old. In 1808, Charles Hardenbergh died, and his heirs decided to auction off his horses, his cattle, and his slaves.

On the day of the auction, Isabella learned from her mother that the family would probably be split up. She was told that she must remember to pray. If she prayed that her masters would be kind, God would make sure that she would be sold to good people.

The family was indeed separated. Isabella was sold to a man named John Nealy, who owned a store and dock in nearby Kingston, New York. Her brother Peter was bought by someone else. Yet no one purchased their father, who was old and badly crippled by rheumatism, so Hardenbergh's heirs considered setting him free.

Almost 30 years earlier, a law had been passed in the state of New York that allowed any slave who was over 50 years old to be freed by his master. However, the law required that the person must be able to earn a living, and the crippled James was unable to work. At last, Hardenbergh's heirs decided to free both

James and Betsey, for she appeared to be young and healthy enough to support both of them. The two were allowed to continue living in their dark cellar.

Separated from her parents, Isabella felt truly alone for the first time in her life. She spoke only Dutch while the Nealys spoke only English. Because she could not understand her mistress's orders, she was frequently beaten. Working for the Nealy family, she later said, was like being in a war.

After Isabella had been living on the Nealy farm for a short while, she heard distressing news: Her mother had become ill and was gradually losing all of her strength. One day, James returned to the cellar after a morning walk and found his wife in a coma. By nightfall, she was dead.

For a while, Isabella's father lived with two other elderly former slaves in a cabin near the Hardenbergh farm. James's housemates soon died, however, and he was left alone. Isabella learned of her father's troubles and obtained permission to visit him. She found him ill and depressed. Hoping to cheer him up, she told him she had heard rumors that a law which would free all of the slaves in New York might soon be passed. If this happened, she said, then she would come and take care of him.

After Isabella returned to the Nealy farm, her master and mistress tried to teach her English. But their teaching met with little success, and they became impatient with their student's slow progress. One Sunday morning, when Isabella was still about 11 years old, they told her to go out to the barn. There she found her master heating some metal rods over re-hot coals. Without offering Isabella any explanation, he grabbed her hands and tied them together. Then he began to beat her with the rods. Although Isabella pleaded with him to stop and called out to God for help, the beating continued until her back was covered with blood.

Isabella's father learned about the brutal punishment that his daughter had received, and he was able to persuade a local fisherman named Martin Schryver to buy her from the Nealys. Schryver, who did not own any other slaves, took her to his farm, which was about five miles from the Nealy's place. He and his wife were rough-mannered, uneducated people who farmed, fished, and ran a tavern. They treated Isabella well, although she felt uncomfortable around the coarse men who visited the tavern.

An industrious worker, Isabella hauled in catches of fish, hoed cornfields, and gathered

roots and herbs for the homemade beer that was sold in the tavern. It was probably during this period in her life that she began to smoke a pipe—a habit that she kept up for many years. She also became relatively fluent in English, although her speech would always be marked by a strong Dutch accent.

Shortly after Isabella was purchased by the Schryvers, she learned that her father had starved to death in his cabin. Everyone in her

Female slaves worked both in the home and in the fields along-side men. By the time Truth reach-ed her early teens, she had shown that she was a strong, reliable worker. Her competence at house-hold tasks would prove valuable to her in later years.

family except for Peter was either dead or a virtual stranger, she realized. In addition, all of her estranged brothers and sisters supposedly lived far away. She now felt very much alone.

Isabella consequently decided that she had only one thing left to pray for: her freedom. Perhaps the rumors were true, she said to herself. Perhaps the slaves in New York would be freed after all.

Chapter Three

Out
of Bondage

ISABELLA WAS OWNED by the Schryvers for only about a year and a half before she was sold once again, in 1810. Schryver greatly valued his hardworking slave, but he was unable to turn down an offer by a local farmer named John Dumont, who purchased Isabella for a price that was three times what Schryver had paid for her.

Isabella's new owner lived with his wife in nearby New Paltz, New York, and had 10 slaves on his large farm. Dumont was patient and relatively kind, but his wife was mean spirited and took an instant dislike to her

A Hudson River community in the early 1800s. When Truth was sold in 1810 to a new master who had a farm near the Hudson, she believed that God would soon free her from her bondage.

Some estate owners increased their profits by encouraging thier slaves to have large families and then selling excess workers to southern slave-trading businesses, such as the one shown here.

quiet-spken new slave. Dumont's wife instructed her two white maids to "lord it over" Isabella and to "grind her down."

Even though Isabella was often badly treated by her mistress and co-workers in the Dumont household, she remembered her mother's instructions to obedient and always tried hard to please her owners. Some of the other slaves on the farm even teased her for being too obedient. But she had been taught to repay evil with good, and she had developed

a deep spiritual belief that her hard work would eventually be rewarded.

Such a rewared seemed to come to her during her middle teens, when she fell in love with a handsome young slave named Robert who lived on a nearby estate. They soon began meeting with each other whenever they had a break from their labors. Although slaves were not U.S. citizens, and therefore could not be legally married, many couples were allowed to live together as man and wife.

Robert's owner, who was named Catlin, opposed the match between his slave and
Isabella. Because Catlin was only interested
in building up his estate, he wanted his female
slaves to bear lots of children whom he could

Disobedient slaves were sometimes savagely punished by their masters. Truth's first love, a young slave named Robert, was beaten senseless for defying his master's orders to stop visiting her.

either sell or put to work in his fields. He ordered Robert to stop meeting with Isabella and instead to take for a wife one of the female slaves on the Catlin estate.

Despite his owner's command, Robert decid-

On July 4, 1827, slaves in New York celebrated Freedom Day— the day on which the state legislature had decreed that all slaves over the age of 28 would be freed. Abolitionist society agents such as the one shown here worked hard for the passage of national emancipation laws.

ed to continue seeing Isabella in secret. Nevertheless, Catlin became suspicious and decided to set a trap for his disobedient slave. One afternoon, Robert was told by another slave that Isabella was sick and needed his help. He immediately stopped working and ran off to see her.

Isabella was actually in fine health; she was working in Dumont's kitchen, unaware that Catlin and his son were hiding in the bushes outside. When she suddenly heard someone scream outside, she went to the window, where she watched in horror as the Catlins beat Robert with heavy sticks. Dumont, who also heard the commotion, ran over to the Catlins and ordered them to stop beating their slave before they killed him. The Catlins yanked Robert to his feet, bound his hands, and marched him away.

Robert survived his terrible beating, but his spirit was broken. Never again did he disobey his master and visit Isabella. Instead, he agreed to take one of the slaves on the Catlin estate to be his wife.

Bitterly disappointed at the outcome of her first romance, Isbella sought comfort through prayer. The religious instruction that she had received from her mother had helped her to become deeply devoted to the principles of love and forgiveness, and she had come to believe that she had a special, very private relationship with Jesus Christ. She began to feel that Jesus was with her at all times as a friend and counselor, and that if she talked to him, he would answer.

By the time Isabella was in her late teens, she had grown tall and strong and had proved that she could work in the fields at least as hard as most men. In fact, some of the other

slaves believed that she was a little bit strange because all she seemed to do was work and pray. Despite their view of her, she enjoyed the company of her co-workers, and she enjoyed listening to the colorful stories that they told around the fireplace in their quarters.

Even in the North, free blacks were never entirely safe from the threat of being kidnapped and transported to the South. Many legally freed slaves were accused of being fugitives and then dragged away in chains by southern slave catchers.

Not long after Isabella's match with Robert had come to an end, she agreed to accept as her husband one of Dumont's older slaves. He was named Thomas, and he had taken two previous wives. Dumont arranged for a black preacher to perform the ceremony for a slave

Known for their devout religious faith and their plain style of dress, the Quakers were strong supporters of the abolitionist movement and often helped to find sanctuary for escaped slaves.

marriage.

Although Isabella and Thomas never became very close, they had a number of children together. Their first child, a girl named Diana, was born in 1815. During the next 12 years, Isabella gave birth to 4 more children: Elizabeth, Hannah, Peter, and Sophie. Each child learned the same lessons from Isabella that she had learned from her own mother: Never steal, never lie, and always obey your master.

While taking on the duties of a mother and a wife, Isabella continued her labors for the Dumonts and found her life complicated by the extra work involved in nursing and caring for her children. Sometimes, she would strap one of her children to her back while she hoed a field. At other times, she would tie an old sheet to the branch of a tree and have one of her older children watch over the younger ones while they played on the makeshift swing. The other slaves on the Dumont farm also helped to raise the children.

Year after year, Isabella panted corn, chopped wood, and hauled buckets of water for the Dumonts. But she never gave up her hope that she would be free one day. In 1824, good news finally reached her. Pressured by abolitionist groups, the New York state legislature had passed an emancipation law requiring that all slaves born before July 4, 1799, be freed on June 4, 1827. Male slaves born after the 4th of July in 1799 were to be emancipated when they were 28 years old, and female slaves were to be freed after their 25th birthday. Although no one knew for sure when Isabella had been born, the Dumonts agreed that she was eligible to be freed in 1827.

Naturally, Isabella was ecstatic that her prayers had finally been answered. She and the other slaves who were born before July 4, 1799, eagerly began to look forward to what became known as "Freedom Day." Then Dumont promised her that he would free her one year earlier than required if she worked especially hard before the time came for her to be released. Isabella accepted his proposal and began to work even longer hours than usual. The other slaves laughed at her for thinking that Dumont would keep his promise, but she was certain that her master would not lie to her.

In 1825, a year before she was to be freed, Isabella received a serious cut in one of her hands during a harvesting accident. The hand became infected and she was not able to work at her usual pace. The fall harvest did not turn out to be a good one for Dumont, and when Isabella asked for her freedom in July 1826, the farmer said that he could not afford to let her go. He also claimed that she had cheated him out of a year's worth of work.

Before Isabella left, she decided to finish a job she had begun: spinning the annual harvest of wool. Because she could not take all of her children with her when she ran away, she wanted to leave on somewhat good terms with

Dumont. However, the Dumont' flock of sheep yielded more wool than usual that year, and by the time she had finished her spinning, it was late in the autumn of 1826.

As Isabella prepared to escape, she began to wonder when would be the best time of the day to leave. Nightime seemed to be the safest time to run away, but she was afraid of the dark. Escaping by daylight would be too dangerous because someone would surely see her.

Isabella prayed to God for guidance, and a solution came to her. She decided that she would leave neither by day nor by night but in between, at dawn. There would be just enough light to calm her fears, while the early hour would ensure that the Dumonts and their neighbors would still be asleep. She told no one—not even Tom or her children—out of fear that her plans would be discovered.

On the morning of her escape, Isabella awoke before dawn, gathered together some food and clothes, and bundled them up inside a large piece of cloth. She then got her baby daughter, Sophie, whom she had decided to take with her. Leaving the other children behind was a difficult thing to do, but she knew that they would be well cared for by the other slaves.

After gaining her freedom, Truth worked as a domestic servant for a Quaker couple who had purchased her and then freed her.

As Isabella walked silently out of the house, the sun was just beginning to light up the sky. By daytime, she was far from her master's house.

Isabella again prayed to God, and again there came an answer to her worries. She walked to the home of a farmer who knew her and asked him for shelter. Although the farmer was ill and could not take her in, he directed her to a Quaker couple named Isaac and Maria Van Wagener who might be willing to hide her. When she reached the Van Wagener house, she was welcomed inside. After hearing her story, the couple immediately offered her a job and a place to stay in their home.

A short time later, Dumont arrived at the Van Wagener house. Confronting Isabella, he threatened her with harsh punishment for running away at night. "I did not run away," she said. "I walked away by daylight."

Wishing to save Isabella from any further grief, Van Wagener offered to buy her and her baby from her owner for a small sum. Dumont could see that she was not going to return with him; he also realized that she would never again be willing to work hard for him. He decided to accept Van Wagener's offer.

Isabella felt extremely grateful to the Van Wageners, and she told them that she would work hard for them. She was told not to think of herself as their slave, for from this day on she was a free woman. "There is but one

master," Van Wagener said, "and He who is your master is my master."

During the next few months, Isabella devoted her energies to repaying the Van Wageners for their kindness. Yet she found

The town of Kingston, New York, was a bustling port on the Hudson River when Truth traveled to the courthouse there to petition for the return of her son, Peter. The boy had been sold by his master and was being raised on a plantation in Alabama.

herself growing homesick for her family and for the spirit of camaraderie that she had enjoyed with the other slaves on the Dumont farm. She was saddened by the knowledge that she could not join her old friends for the

Freedom Day celebrations on July 4, 1827. She also felt sad for her children at the Dumont farm. They were still slaves (unlike Sophie) and would have to wait until their term of service with Dumont was finished before they were freed.

Isabella became even more troubled shortly thereafter, when the news reached her that Dumont had sold her son, Peter, to a man named Solomon Gedney, who had then given the boy to his brother-in-law, an Alabama plantation owner named Fowler. Isabella was especially alarmed because Alabama did not have any emancipation laws. Peter would remain a slave forever if he was not rescued from Fowler's plantation.

Determined to have Peter returned to New York, Isabella went to the Dumonts and pleaded with them to buy back her son. Dumont was somewhat sympathetic, telling her he had not known that Peter would be taken south. However, his wife merely laughed at her and asked her why she was making such a fuss over just one child. "I'll have my child again," Isabella said. Even though she did not have any money and therefore was unable to buy back her son, she insisted, "God has enough, or what's better."

Isabella next visited the mother of Solomon

Gedney, hoping that the woman would take pity and tell her son to have Peter brought back from Alabama. However, Gedney's mother was unmoved by Isabella's story and refused to help.

A dejected Isabella then received advice from friends who told her that New York's emancipation law expressly forbade slaveowners from transporting their slaves out of the state. Although free blacks such as Isabella could not file a lawsuit in some states, New York permitted them to do so. Under the advice of a group of Quakers who often helped former slaves, she traveled to Kingston, the local seat of the government, and filed a lawsuit against Solomon Gedney for selling Peter to an out-of-state resident.

A grand jury heard Isabella's case and decided in her favor. She was given a writ, or legal document, that the local law officer was to serve to Solomon Gedney. The writ ordered Gedney to appear before the court with Peter so that a jury could decide on whether or not the boy should be returned to his mother.

Late in the fall of 1827, Gedney left for Alabama, and he returned the following spring with Peter. But Gedney had no intention of giving the boy back to his mother. Gedney's defiance frustrated Isabella and prompted her

LADIES' DEPARTMENT.

"Am I not a Woman and a Sister?"

White Lady, happy, proud and free,
Lend awhile thine ear to me ;
Let the Negro Mother's wail
Turn thy pale cheek still more pale.
Can the Negro Mother joy
Over this her captive boy,
Which in bondage and in tears,
For a life of wo she rears?
Though she bears a Mother's name,
A Mother's rights she may not claim ;
For the white man's will can part,
Her darling from her bursting heart.

From the Genius of Universal Emancipation.
LETTERS ON SLAVERY.—No. III.

The abolitionist newspaper Emancipator *printed this poem about a black mother's appeal to end the cruel system that allowed masters to take young children away from their parents.*

to persuade the New Paltz constable to serve the writ again. Before long, Gedney appeared in the Kingston court and agreed to appear at a hearing that would decide Peter's fate. Isabella hoped for a quick decision, but she was soon disappointed. A judge postponed the hearing for several months.

A friend advised Isabella to contact a local

lawyer for assistance. After the lawyer listened to Isabella tell her story, he said to her that
he could obtain her son's release within 24
hours. But first she had to pay him a fee of
five dollars.

Isabella did not have that amount of money,
but she believed that her Quaker friends would
lend her the sum. All in the same day, she
traveled about 10 miles to borrow money from
the Quakers and then brought it to the
lawyer's office. On the following day, the
lawyer called upon Isabella at the Van
Wageners' house. He said that there was a problem, although he still thought that he could
free Peter, as promised. The boy claimed that
he did not know who his mother was and that
he wanted to stay with Gedney. Isabella would
have to appear before a judge and prove to him
that she was indeed Peter's mother.

When the day of the hearing finally arrived, Isabella walked into the judge's chambers
and saw Peter standing among the court officers. She held out her arms to embrace him,
but he ran away from her and cried out for his
master. The judge banged his gavel for order,
then turned to Isabella and asked her she was
really the boy's mother. She swore that she
was his mother, adding that Peter was
frightened by all of the people around him. The

judge ultimately ruled that Gedney had violated a state law by allowing Peter to be taken out of New York, and so he had to give up ownership of the boy.

At first, Peter kicked and screamed and did not seem at all happy that he was being returned to his mother. However, after he had settled down, he admitted to Isabella that she looked like his mother. When she asked him why he had not said so earlier, the boy told her that Gedney had threatened to beat him if he acknowledged her as his mother. Isabella later

Following the court's decision to grant Truth custody of her son, she could take pride in the fact that she was one of the first black women in the United States to win a lawsuit. Shown here is the Kingston courthouse in which the case was heard.

found that Peter's entire body was covered with scars from whippings that he had received while he was on the Fowler plantation.

With Peter in tow, saved from a life of slavery in the South, Isabella walked proudly out of the Kingston courthouse. With little but her courage and faith in God to guide her, she had just become one of the first black women in the country to win a court case. After having been a slave for nearly 30 years, she was now beginning to enjoy some of the rewards that came with being free.

Chapter Four

A
True
Believer

AFTER ISABELLA GAINED her freedom, she worked as a maid for the Van Wageners for two years. Gradually, she began to grow a little dissatisfied with her sheltered life with the Quaker couple. By 1828, she was hoping that she could someday buy a home where her children could live, and she knew that to fulfill her dreams she must leave the Van Wageners and find a well-paying job as a house servant.

Since servants in New Paltz received fairly low wages, Isabella listened intently whenever she heard about high-paying jobs that were available in New York City. Many former slaves

In 1828, Truth moved to New York City with her son, Peter. They were amazed by the city's sprawling network of streets and busy commercial atmosphere. This engraving shows Five Points, one of the city's most ethnically diverse neighborhoods in the 1800s.

Finding steady employment as a servant in the homes of wealthy New Yorkers, Truth was at last able to set aside some money for the house she was hoping to buy for her family. The artist of the illustration shown here sketched Truth as she was scrubbing clothes.

who had worked on farms in upstate New York were leaving the area in search of job opportunities in port cities along the East Coast and in the rapidly growing West. Although Isabella knew that she could earn more money in a large city than in a rural environment, she was reluctant to move away from her children, three of whom were still bound to the Dumonts.

By this time, some of the circumstances in Isabella's personal life had changed significantly since she had left the Dumonts. Her husband, Thomas, had been emancipated on Freedom Day and had moved to New Paltz, where he worked at various jobs. Although he lived in the same area as Isabella, she rarely saw him anymore; they had agreed to go their separate ways.

Another of the changes in Isabella's life involved her relationship with the Dumonts. She and the Dumonts had settled their differences, and she had become a frequent visitor to their home. She even left Sophie with her other children on the Dumont farm while she stayed in Kingston, while trying to win Peter's freedom (she supported herself there by working as a servant, and it would have been awkward for her to have a child accompanying her shile she worked).

Isabella also became involved in the church. She had previously considered her religious faith to be a personal matter that she could not share with others. As a slave, she had been separated from many of the people who were dearest to her, and she was still afraid that Jesus Christ would somehow be stolen from her, too. Yet she could not resist the lure of the beautiful hymns that she heard when she

walked by the local Methodist church.

The friendliness of the congregation also encouraged Isabella to accept an invitation to join the Methodist church. At that time, most churches required blacks to sit in special sections, often in the balconies above the main area. However, Isabella's church was free of such discriminatory practices, and many of its

For a short while, Truth attended Sunday services at the John Street Methodist Church (shown here). She stopped going there because of the church's policy of segregating its black and white members.

members took a strong interest in her.

Among Isabella's friends at church was Miss Gear, a schoolteacher who was planning to move to New York City. The woman offered to find work there for Isabella, who decided that it was finally time to leave New Paltz. After visiting her daughters—of whom the oldest, Diana, was 13—Isabella packed her

bags and said good-bye to the Van Wageners. Peter accompanied her so that he could learn a trade in the city.

In the summer of 1828, Isabella and Peter boarded a ship for the journey down the Hudson River to New York City, which had already become the country's leading port and com-

Determined to do something to help relieve the suffering of the poor, Truth became a volunteer worker at a women's shelter called the Magdalene Asylum. The Bowery Hill section in New York where the shelter was located is shown here as it appeared in 1831.

mercial center. Used to the farms, small towns, and forests of Ulster County, Isabella and Peter found the city both intriguing and frightening. They were impressed by the tremendous activity around the dock areas and by the city's broad, cobblestone avenues and tall buildings. However, they were shock-

ed to see how many poor people crowded the slum areas. Thousands of new immigrants—many of them from Ireland—were arriving in the city each year, and great numbers of them went unemployed and hungry.

Eventualy, Isabella and Peter became settled in the city, joining the swelling number of former slaves who had come to New York to find jobs in the city's shipping and manufac-

In 1832, Truth joined a religious community founded by the mystic preachers Robert Matthews and Elijah Pierson near Ossining, New York (shown here). The two self-proclaimed prophets called their commune the Kingdom and declared, "Our creed is truth."

turing industries. With the help of Gear, Isabella soon found steady, well-paying jobs as a servant in the houses of New York merchants. She received part of her payment in the form of room and board. Peter enrolled in a navigation trade school, where he was to undergo training for a job as a seaman or ship's officer.

Before long, Isabella began to hunt for a

religious congregation that she could join. She had noticed many impressive-looking churches upon her arrival, but they either restricted their membership to whites or maintained separate sections for blacks. Because she refused to sit in a church with segregated prayer rooms, she decided to join a black church known as the Zion African Church.

During their meetings, members of the Zion African Church were encouraged to testify about their religious feelings. Isabella soon became well known for giving loud and vigorous expressions of her spiritual faith. She also became noted for her ability to recite passages from the Bible as well as for composing clever sermons.

In addition to attending the Zion African Church, Isabella accepted an invitation from Gear to join a women's evangelical group that walked throughout the city singing hymns to the poor. Isabella soon grew dissatisfied with the evangelists because she believed that they were not doing anything to relieve the suffering of the poor. She left the group and instead devoted her free time to the homeless young women who stayed at this shelter some of them had been rescued from prostitution. Isabella taught them how to cook, sew, and clean house as well as other skills that would help them to find work as servants.

The director of the Magdalene Asylum was Elijah Pierson, a self-proclaimed minister. He had been a merchant until he underwent an intense spiritual experience and became deeply religious. Then he and his wife, Sarah, sold their home and bought a meetinghouse in the Bowery Hill section of New York City, where they conducted prayer sessions with other people who shared their strong religious faith.

The Piersons soon became noted for their somewhat eccentric religious practices, which included going without food or water for four or more days at a time while conducting long prayer sessions. They hoped that their suffering would win favor in God's eyes, and they advised their followers to purify themselves as well by engaging in long fasts. Among their converts was Isabella, who greatly admired the kindly director of the Magdalene Asylum.

Isabella believed that Pierson was a man of great spiritual powers whom God had chosen to relieve the wretchedness of the poor in New York City. After listening to his sermons, she resolved to follow the regimen of fasting that he said would bring light to her spirit. However, fasting was a dangerous practice for a hard working person such as Isabella. After the third day of her fast, she collapsed and subsequently gave up fasting as a way of winning God's favor.

For Pierson's wife, the realization that fasting could be dangerous came too late. In June 1830, she died after a prolonged fast. Her illness and death deeply affected her husband. Convinced that he had become endowed with supernatural powers, he called his congregation together after his wife's death and attempted to bring her back to life through prayer. After this attempt failed, he claimed that devine powers had chosen him to form an earthly kingdom of God in New York. He announced that he should henceforth be called Elijah the Tishbite, a name which sounded like that of a biblical prophet.

Isabella, who also believed that she could communicate directly with God, was mesmerized by Pierson. He seemed to her to be like one of the holy men in the Bible. In August 1831, she moved into the meeting house and became a full-time servant for Pierson and a devout follower of his religious sect.

The attraction that Isabella felt for a mystical religious faith was shared by many other Americans at that time. Religious groups such as the Mormons, a denomination that formed in central New York in the 1820s, believed that divine revelation had been given

The Kingdom became embroiled in controversy after Pierson died and Matthews was charged with murdering his fellow prophet. Eager to learn more about the scandal-ridden commune, many New Yorkers rushed to buy the boook written about Matthews by his estranged wife.

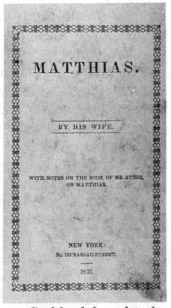

MATTHIAS.

BY HIS WIFE.

WITH NOTES ON THE BOOK OF MR. STONE, ON MATTHIAS.

NEW YORK:
No. 130 NASSAU STREET.

1835.

to certain people whom God had found to be especially holy. Many Americans attended emotional religious gatherings known as revival meetings, where congregants testified about their spiritual faith and listened to sermons by traveling preachers.

Among those who claimed to possess unusual God-given powers was a man from Albany, New York, named Robert Matthews. Believing himself to be a prophet of biblical stature, he renamed himself Mathias, left his wife and children, and began preaching that God was going to destroy the people of Albany for their sinfulness. He then left his hometown and began to travel throughout the state of New York, preaching the word of the Bible and forgiving sins in exchange for money.

One day in May 1832, Isabella opened the door of the meeting house and was startled to find a long-bearded figure in a flowing robe standing before her. The man asked to see Elijah the Tishbite, telling her, "I am Matthias. I am God the Father and have the power to do all things." He wore his beard long because he believed that no man who shaved could be a true Christian.

Pierson and Matthews soon found that they had much in common. Matthews stayed at the meeting house, and Pierson bought his fellow prophet a horse and carriage so that he could convey himself around the city in proper style. In 1832, the two men decided to found a religious community on a farm owned by a married couple named Benjamin and Ann Folger. The farm was situated near the Hudson River, about 30 miles north of New York City. The Folgers and their family were the only ones besides Isabella who joined Pierson and Matthews at the community, which they called Zion Hill (it also became known as the Kingdom). Isabella contributed her life savings to the commune, as did everyone else except

Matthews, who claimed that he did not have any money.

For a while, the members of the Kingdom lived in harmony. Then Matthews began to exert complete control over the community, and his unusual teachings caused tensions within the group. He claimed that every person had a soul which might or might not have a spiritual bond with the soul of another person, meaning that only people with matched souls should marry and have sexual relations.

After somehow determining that Ann Folger's soul did not match her husband's, Matthews issued her a divorce (even though he did not have the legal power to do so) and married her himself. Benjamin Folger became extremely upset over these acts and began to feud with Matthews. In addition, Matthews refused to let Pierson be examined by a doctor after he became seriously ill. Matthews claimed that God did not mean for the people of the Kingdom to need medical help.

Isabella soon became disillusioned with the Kingdom, whose members just seemed to spend their days bickering or engaging in strange religious rituals, leaving her to do all of the work. Knowing that no one could match her own strong spirit, which was in God's possession, she refused to take part in Mat-

THE PROPHET!

A

FULL AND ACCURATE REPORT

OF THE

JUDICIAL PROCEEDINGS

IN THE

EXTRAORDINARY AND HIGHLY INTERESTING CASE

OF

MATTHEWS, *alias* MATTHIAS,

CHARGED WITH HAVING

Swindled Mr. B. H. Folger,

OF THE CITY OF NEW-YORK,

OUT OF CONSIDERABLE PROPERTY:

WITH THE

Speeches of Counsel, and Opinion of the Court on the motion of the District Attorney, that a Nolle Prosequi be entered in the Case.

ALSO,

A Sketch of the Impostor's Character,

And a detailed History of his Career as a "Prophet," together with many other Particulars, which have not hitherto been published.

BY W. E. DRAKE, CONGRESSIONAL AND LAW REPORTER.

NEW-YORK: PRINTED AND PUBLISHED BY W. MITCHELL, 265 BOWERY, And may be had of him, and all the Booksellers.

1834.

Price Six Cents.

thews's practice of matching souls. She was also beginning to feel that she had to do something about her son, Peter, who had dropped out of school and was becoming a delinquent.

In August 1834, Isabella decided to leave the commune. She returned to New York City and made arrangements to work for one of her former employers, the Whitings. She then returned to Zion Hill to pack up her belongings and discovered that Pierson had died in her absence.

A scandal soon erupted at Zion Hill. Pierson's relatives accused Matthews of poisoning his fellow prophet and of stealing his money. And even though the doctors who examined Pierson's body did not find any traces of poison in it, Matthews was arrested for murder. Isabella was implicated in the alleged murder plot although she was not officially charged with any crime.

Matthew's murder trial became one of the chief topics of conversation on the streets of New York City. Three different books were published about the Kingdom commune, helping to circulate rumors that the commune

---

One of the founding members of the Kingdom, Benjamin Folger published a book and a newspaper account about the commune. In them he accused Matthews of being a swindler and Truth of being an evil witch. Truth sued him for slander and was awarded $125 in damages.

Following the breakup of the Kingdom, Truth returned to New York City, where she worked as a house servant until 1843. This engraving of Hanover Square is from the 1830s.

members had engaged in all sorts of shocking behavior. In April 1835, Matthews was found to be not guilty. Nevertheless, the commune disbanded soon after he was acquitted.

Even though Isabella had settled into a quiet life in New York City while working for the Whitings, she was unable to escape the controversy that surrounded the Kingdom. A New York newspaper printed a sensationalized account of life on the commune based on information provided by Benjamin Folger. The story accused Isabella of being an evil witch who had single-handedly destroyed the peace and harmony that had once existed at Zion

Hill.

Hurt by this story, Isabella collected letters from former employers that testified about her high moral character. Yet she was still met in public with scorn. Fortunately for her, a newspaper reporter named Gilbert Vale grew interested in her case and invited her to tell her side of the story. Vale's account of the Kingdom, "The Narrative of Isabella, or Fanaticism: Its Source and Influence," helped to restore Isabella's reputation by inviting the public to view her as the victim of the insane plans of Pierson and Matthews.

Encouraged by Vale and other supporters, Isabella decided to file a lawsuit against Folger and the newspaper that had printed the slanderous article about her. She won her case and received $125 in damages from the defendants. She also learned from this entire experience to look at self-proclaimed religious leaders with a more critical eye than she had done in the past.

Isabella spent the next eight years in New York City as a servant for the Whitings. She still hoped to save enough money to buy a house in which her family could be reunited. However, a family reunion did not seem to be in her future. Her daughters remained on the Dumont farm until their terms of service were over and then they looked for work away from New York City; her son, Peter, was arrested on numerous occasions for vandalism before enlisting as a sailor on a merchant vessel. Isabella received several letters from him before their correspondence ended for good in 1841.

By 1843, Isabella had begun to believe that New York City was a dangerous place for blacks. Slave catchers roamed the streets, looking for slaves who had escaped from the South. Along with the recaptured slaves, a number of free blacks were kidnapped and smuggled out of the city and into slavery. The growing competition for jobs between blacks and European immigrants also made life increasingly difficult for blacks, who faced severe discrimination and became the victims of occasional outbreaks of racial violence.

As Isabella began to dream of starting a new life away from New York City, she realized that her experiences as a slave, mother, and devout Christian had given her a perspective on human rights and spiritual well-being that she wanted to share with others. She spoke to God constantly, and he affirmed this realization. In her own mind, she heard powerful voices telling her that she had a mission to help the needy and the oppressed.

During the early 1840s, Truth began to feel that God was calling upon her to share her spiritual faith with people throughout the country.

Early in the summer of 1843, Isabella decided to act on God's command that she leave New York City and become a traveling preacher. Although she was unsure of what lay ahead, she excitedly made preparations for the journey. A true believer, she was confident that He would make good use of her.

Chapter Five

God's Pilgrim

WHEN THE FIRST bit of sunlight illuminated the sky over New York City on June 1, 1843, Isabella was already awake, stuffing a few dresses into an old pillowcase. The day of her departure had come at last. Her employers, the Whitings, were stunned by the news that she was leaving and asked her where she would be staying. "The Lord is going to give me a new home," Isabella told them, "and I am going away." Hoisting her pillowcase over her shoulder, she said, "Farewell, friends, I must be about my Father's business."

Heading east, in the direction that an inner

When Truth was in her mid-forties, she decided to take up the hard life of a traveling preacher. Asking God to give her "a name with a handle" for her new vocations, she received a message to change her name from Isabella to Sojourner Truth.

voice had told her to follow, Isabella took a ferry to Brooklyn. There she disembarked and began walking on a road that stretched eastward, toward Long Island. At age 46, she felt free, as though she were repeating the escape from slavery that she had made nearly 17 years before.

However, something still bothered Isabella. She believed that the name she had been given as a slave was inappropriate for a person who was beginning a new life as God's pilgrim. She wanted a new name, a free woman's name.

Calling on God for help in choosing her new name, Isabella received an answer: She should call herself "Sojourner." She thought that it was a good name for someone who had been called on, she later said, to "travel up and

In June 1843, Truth boarded a ferry at the downtown New York docks and began her travels as a preacher. She soon gained renown for her inspiring sermons, which she began with the announcement, "Children, I talk to God and God talks to me."

down the land, showing the people their sins, and being a sign unto them." The name also reminded her of the holy people described in the Bible who had traveled to foreign lands to preach the word of God. More and more, she felt as though she was following in the tradition of the great prophets of biblical times.

Proudly bearing her new name, Sojourner continued walking for another few miles, until she saw a woman working in front of a house. Having grown thirsty, Sojourner asked her for some water. As the woman was gladly fulfilling Sojourner's request, she asked the traveler what her name was.

When Sojourner told her, the woman attempted to find out what Sojourner's last name was and asked, "Sojourner what?" Her name was simply Sojourner, the traveler said, and then she continued on her journey. Yet the woman's question continued to nag at her. Why did she not have a last name?

Once again, Sojourner prayed for guidance. And once more, an answer came to her: Truth. Her full name would be Sojourner Truth—a very suitable name for one of God's pilgrims, she thought.

As Truth traveled east across Long Island, she preached in the farms and villages through which she passed. The white farmers whom she encountered stopped their work to listen to her, finding themselves enthralled by the powerful and inspiring manner in which she spoke. They were amazed that she seemed to know every word in the Bible even though she was illiterate.

During these travels, Truth was often invited to stay with the people who had gathered to hear her speak. To repay them for their kindness in providing her with food and shelter, she would wash their clothes or scrub their floors. Word about the fiery preacher spread throughout Long Island. People began to whisper, "It must be Sojourner Truth" whenever she appeared at a religious meeting in a new neighborhood.

Eventually, Truth decided that she should

In the fall of 1843, Truth joined a cooperative community in Northampton, Massachusetts. One of the community's leader was abolitionist speaker Samuel Hill.

follow God's call by heading to another area. She took a ship across Long Island Sound and proceeded northward, preaching in Connecticut and Massachusetts. Wherever she went, people flocked to listen to her.

Truth eventually arrived in Northampton, a town located along the Connecticut River in the heart of Massachusetts. There she visited the Northampton Association of Education and Industry, a cooperative community that operated a silkworm farm. The community members shared equally in all of the work but did not participate in any of the religious fanaticism that had existed in Robert Mat-

thews's Kingdom commune. Attracted by the Northampton Association's idealism and spirit of good fellowship, Truth joined the community in late 1843.

Because she held strict moral views, Truth had difficulty in accepting some of the tenets put forth by many of her associates when they engaged in free-thinking debates. *"Three-thirds* of the people here are wrong," she once

Truth was among the members of the Northampton Association of Education and Industry who operated a silk-manufacturing business in this factory building.

stated at a community meeting, unaware that her figure included everyone at Northampton. In spite of being criticized by her, the community members admired Truth for her keen intellect and forthright manner. They respected her even more after she confronted a mob of young men who were disrupting a community religious meeting. The young men were so entranced by her voice that they agreed to leave only if she sang some hymns for them.

While Truth was living at the community, she met many prominent public figures. Among the people who either lived in the community or came to visit the Northampton Asociation were abolitionists Samuel Hill, George Benson, and David Ruggles, as well as two of the leading organizers and speakers of the anti-slavery movement, William Lloyd Garrison and Frederick Douglass. Although the importation of slaves into the United States was forbidden after 1808, slavery was still being practiced in most of the southern states. Led by Garrison and Douglass, the abolitionist movement sought to put an end to slavery.

In 1831, Garrison had founded an influential antislavery newspaper, the *Liberator,* and he had formed the New England Anti-Slavery Society during the following year. Douglass, who had escaped from slavery in 1838, was just beginning to enjoy his reputation as one of the most eloquent abolitionist lecturers. Truth was greatly impressed by the effectiveness of these activists in stirring up antislavery sentiment in the North.

By 1846, the Northampton Association had disbanded, and Truth took up housekeeping work for George Benson and other abolitionist

William Lloyd Garriason led the American Anti-Slavery Society and was the editor of the militant antislavery newspaper, the Liberator. Impressed by Truth's speaking abilities, he urged her to become a traveling lecturer for his organization.

organizers in the area. She also made a trip back to New Paltz to visit her daughter Diana, who had continued working at the Dumont farm after she was freed. While Truth was there, she was gratified to hear that her old master John Dumont had expressed repentance for his past actions. He now said, "Slavery is the wickedest thing in the world."

Between 1846 and 1850, Truth became increasingly involved in the antislavery crusade.

As often happens in many social and political movements, there were many differences of opinion among abolitionist about which methods should be used to bring about an end to slavery in America. For the most part, Truth avoided these disputes, although she did associate more with Garrison's American Anti-Slavery Society than with its rival organization, the less militant American and Foreign Anti-Slavery Society.

Garrison's organization distrusted political parties and stated that slavery could be destroyed only by moral persuasion. The Garrisonians believed that accounts of the cruelties of the slave system printed in abolitionist newspapers would eventually compel the slaveholders to change their ways. The American and Foreign Anti-Slavery Society, on the other hand, cooperated with the Liberty party, the Free Soil party, and other progressive political organizations in working for national laws that would outlaw slavery.

In the late 1830s, a number of autobiographies by former slaves were published in the United States. The writers received encouragement and financial help from antislavery societies, which hoped that the slave narratives would arouse widespread sympathy for the abolitionist cause and dispel the myths that surrounded the issue of slavery. Many Americans mistakenly believed that slaves were content with their condition and were well cared for by their masters.

By the early 1850s, many slave narratives had caught the public's attention, including works by William Wells Brown, Josiah Henson, Solomon Northup, and Samuel Ringgold Ward. The most widely read of these books was *The Narrative of Frederick Douglass,* which was published in 1845, at a time when the abolitionist leader was still a fugitive slave. These books not only presented the unvarnished truth about the brutal slave system, but they also gave stirring accounts of the courage and dignity of slaves who had escaped from bondage. Some of the slave narratives became best-sellers, and they helped to arouse a growing feeling of moral revulsion against slavery among Northerners.

Olive Gilbert, an abolitionist friend of Truth's from Northampton, had been suggesting to Truth since 1847 that she dictate her story. Autobiographical accounts by black women were rare, and Gilbert believed that a narrative of Truth's early life as a slave in the North and her profound faith in God would be uplifting to many people. Truth liked the idea, and in 1850, she and Gilbert published *The*

Narrative of Sojourner Truth, which included an introduction by Garrison. Truth, who could not read the account of her own life, was able to support herself by selling copies of the book at abolitionist meetings.

The fight against slavery was not the only cause to which Truth was attracted. During her stay at the Northampton Association, she had heard lecturers who advocated that women be given the same political and legal

American abolitionist leaders worked hard to build an international antislavery movement. In 1840, delegates from many different countries held debates at the Convention of the World Anti-Slavery Society in London, England.

rights enjoyed by men. Recognizing that she and the women's rights speakers were kindred spirits, Truth decided to join their ranks in yet another battle for freedom. After all, she had struggled against the double burden of being both black and female in a society that imposed severe restrictions on both groups for nearly 50 years.

In the 1840s, women in the United States enjoyed few rights. They could not vote or hold political office. They were paid far less than male workers. And if they were lucky enough to receive an education, they were usually taught in a classroom separate from the male students.

When a woman married, her property and earnings fell under her husband's control. She was not allowed to sue him for a divorce, yet he could divorce her; and in such cases, she was not permitted to testify against him. In the event of a divorce, the husband was given the right to retain custody of the children. As a crowning indignity, women were told by ministers and priests that God looked upon them as being inferior to men.

The first significant opposition to this state of affairs in the United States was organized by women such as Lucy Stone, Susan B. Anthony, and Angelina and Sarah Grimké, who had earlier worked to help abolish slavery. As participants in the abolitionist struggle, they had become veterans at organizing meetings, collecting signatures for petitions, and speaking in public. Lucretia Mott and some of the other pioneer feminists also worked in the underground railroad, helping runaway slaves from the South escape to the northern states, Canada, or Mexico. The women's rights advocates had come to see that national laws must be challenged when they violate a higher moral law.

Many women abolitionists compared the plight of women in America to that of slaves in the South and declared that both women and slaves must be liberated. The comparison was somewhat valid because even though white women possessed some rights, neither women nor slaves were free to enjoy all of the rights promised to American citizens in the U.S. Constitution. Truth had long ago recognized the similarities between the condition of women and slaves in the United States, and her speeches at abolitionist meetings forcefully pointed out that she continued to be oppressed even after she had become a free woman.

Not all of the male members of the antislavery movement agreed with Truth and the other women abolitonists on the issue of women's equality. Garrison and Douglass were avid supporters of women's rights, but many other abolitionists remained unsympathetic to the feminist cause and did not want to allow women to assume leadership roles in antislavery societies. The prominent abolitionist spokesman Lewis Tappan stated his displeasure at the election of Lucretia Mott and other women to the executive committee

of the American Anti-Slavery Society by declaring, "To put a woman on the committee with men is against the usages of civilized society."

The women abolitionists reacted to the shabby treatment accorded them by many of the anti-slavery movement's leaders by pushing even harder to promote the cause of women's rights. A turning point occurred in 1840, at

Vilified by southern newspapers, abolitionist society agents were sometimes viewed as troublemakers in the North, too. In 1835, a hostile mob in Boston, Massachusetts, dragged William Lloyd Garrison through the streets when he attempted to make an antislavery speech.

the World Anti-slavery Convention held in London, England, when Elizabeth Cady Stanton, Lucretia Mott, and other American women delegates were forbidden by the convention committee from sitting in the same section as their male colleagues. The women were infuriated, and they returned to the United States determined to fight for legal equality.

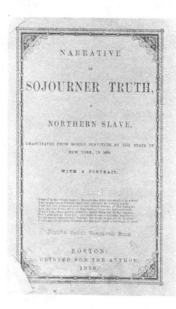

In 1850, Truth published her autobiograhy, a rare accomplshment for a black woman at that time. Having never learned how to read or write, she dictated the narrative of her life to an abolitionist friend.

During the next seven years, the women's movement attracted many supporters and held a number of meetings. In 1848, feminists organized the first national women's rights conference at a church in Seneca Falls, New York. Hundreds of female activists were joined by a courageous group of men who supported women's equality. Disregarding the jeers of anti-feminist men in the audience, the delegates issued a Declaration of Sentiments and Resolutions, a document based to a great extent on the Declaration of Independence. The declaration proposed an 11-point plan for

Susan B. Anthony was one of the early leaders of the women's rights movement. She later published a newspaper entitled The Revolution, *whose motto was "The true republic— men, their rights and nothing more; women, their rights and nothing less."*

helping women achieve equality with men.

Truth did not attend the 1848 convention, but she went to many other women's rights meetings. In October 1850, she traveled to Worcester, Massachusetts, to speak at that year's national women's rights convention. There she listened—along with a thousand others—to such distinguished speakers as Stanton, Mott, Stone, Douglass, and Garrison.

At last, Truth was called on to speak. "Sisters," she began, "I ain't clear what you'd be after. If women want any rights more than they's got, why don't they just take them, and not be talking about it?"

However, the problem of attaining equal rights for women was more complex than Truth was willing to admit at the convention. The chief problem was that a sizable number of men strongly opposed equality for women was more complex than Truth was willing to admit at the convention. The chief problem was that a sizable number of men strongly opposed equality for women and were ready to fight to preserve the status quo. In addition, the women's rights activists disagreed among themselves about the best way to achieve their goals. Some wanted to pursue their rights in

A New York City women's rights congress. Truth electrified the audience at an 1850 women's rights convention when she said, "If women want any rights more than they's got, why don't they just take them, and not be talking about it?"

law courts, while others believed that putting pressure on political parties and congressmen would achieve better results. The debates would continue for years at annual conventions held throughout the country.

Yet Truth's defiant message at the 1850 women's rights convention heartened the ranks of nation's abolitionists and feminists as well as all of the oppressed people who yearned for equality. "Why not just take your rights?" she had asked. Many Americans who were deprived of their rights in their own land were beginning to ask the same question.

Chapter Six

Calling Cards

SOJOURNER TRUTH BECAME a well-known figure in both the anti-slavery and women's rights movements after her autobiography was published in 1850. William Lloyd Garrison and his associate Wendell Phillips persuaded her to lend her splended voice to the abolitionist cause, and she soon began traveling with other lecturers on tours throughout New England. While traveling on the lecture circuit, she sold many copies of her book, and with proceeds from the sales, she bought a house in Northampton.

By the time Truth joined the lecture circuit,

During the 1850s, the increasingly heated debate over slavery drew thousands of people to abolitionist conventions. Truth became a lecturer for the American Anti-Slavery Society before deciding to strike out on her own.

From the mid-1810s until the end of the Civil War, abolitionist journals kept up a steady attack on the evils of slavery and called attention to the moral conflicts that the slave system posed for a supposedly democratic and freedom-loving nation.

she looked much older than her 53 years. Her black hair had turned gray, her forehead had become deeply creased, and she wore metal-rimmed glasses to compensate for her fading eyesight. She almost always wore a plain black dress and a long white shawl, with a handkerchief wrapped around her head to make a turban. From her appearance, some people guessed that she was in her 90s.

Consequently, the crowds at abolitionist meetings were astounded by the vigor with which the elderly-looking Truth attacked the institution of slavery. In her lectures, she denounced slaveowners as sinners who would feel the wrath of God someday soon. Few of the people in the mainly white audiences had ever heard a black person other than Frederick Douglass give a public address, and for them it was enlightening to hear a black woman give her views about slavery.

Truth soon became known for her simple but moving anti-slavery speeches and her witty, biting attacks on the hypocrisy of people who owned slaves and yet professed to be Christians. She knew that many Northerners wanted to avoid the issue of slavery and pretended that it was strictly a southern problem. To these people, the millions of wretched black slaves were virtually invisible. Truth believed that it was her mission to force all Americans to confront what she felt was a nationwide moral problem.

During the same year that Truth's narrative began circulating throughout the North, Americans became embroiled in a new conflict over the spread of slavery into the nation's vast territories west of the Mississippi River. Southerners did not want any restrictions plac-

ed on slavery in the West, while Northerners
wanted the territories to be formed into "free
states" where slavery would be forbidden.
Although Congress had previously established a boundary in the West that divided the
region into slave and free territories, the question arose as to whether slavery would be
allowed in the region stretching from Texas to
California that had recently been taken from

One of the most successful "conductors" on the Underground Railroad, Harriet Tubman (left) led more than 300 slaves out of the South to freedom in the North and Canada. A noted abolitionist speaker, she once boasted, "I never run my train off the track, and I never lost a passenger."

Mexico.

In 1850, Congress passed an act called the Compromise of 1850 that divided the southwestern territories into free and slave areas. The act allowed California, which became the nation's second largest state in terms of total area, to enter the Union as a free state. To appease militant legislators in the South who were upset at such a large

SOJOURNER'S MIRROR.

AIR—"AULD LANG SYNE."

Sojourner Truth,

Interested an audience in New Lisbon, Ohio, at the Methodist Episcopal Church, very much, for near an hour, in talking of slavery in this country, and the suffering and injustice inseparable from it. If earnestness is eloquence—and it is—she has a just claim in that appellation, for she makes some powerful appeals which cannot but strike a chord of sympathy in every human heart.

A friend who was present addressed the following lines to the Editor of the *Aurora*.

She pleadeth for her people,
A poor, down-trodden race,
Who dwell in Freedom's boasted land,
With no abiding place.

She pleads that her people
May have their rights restored,
For they have long been toiling,
And yet had no reward.

They are forced the crops to culture,
But not for them they yield,
Although both late and early
They labor in the field.

While she bears upon her body
The scars of many a gash,
She pleadeth for her people
That groan beneath the lash.

She is pleading for the mothers
Who gaze in wild despair
Upon the hated auction-block,
And see their children there.

She feels for those in bondage—
Well may she feel for them;
She knows how fiendish hearts can be
That sell their fellow-men.

Yet those oppressors, steeped in guilt,
She still would have them live,
For she has learned of Jesus
To suffer and forgive.

She wants no carnal weapons,
No engin'ry of death;
She loveth not to hear the sound
Of war's tempestuous breath.

She does not ask you to engage
In death and bloody strife;
She does not dare insult her God
By asking for their life.

But while your kindest sympathies
To foreign lands do roam,
She would ask you to remember
Your own oppressed at home.

She pleads with you to sympathize
With sighs, and groans, and scars,
And note how base the tyranny
Beneath the stripes and stars.

Sojourner's Favorite Song.

We are going home, we have visions bright
Of that holy land, that world of light
Where the long dark night is past,
And the morning of eternity has come at last,
Where the weary Saints no more shall roam,
But dwell in a sunny, and peaceful home,
Where the brow, celestial gems shall crown
And waves of bliss are dashing round.

Chorus—Oh! that beautiful home—oh! that beautiful world.

We are going home, we soon shall be
Where the sky is clear and the soil is free,
Where the victor's song floats over the plains,
And the Seraphs anthem blends with the strains,
Where the sun rolls down his brilliant flood
And beams on a world all fair and good,
And the stars that shone on nature's dome
Will sparkle and dance o'er the spirits home.

Chorus.

The tears and sighs, which here were given,
Exchanged for the glad songs of heaven,
The beauteous forms that sing and shine
And guarded well, by a hand divine,
Pure love and friendship joined
Are waving above that princely band,
And the glory of God, like a molten sea,
Shall bathe that immortal company.

Chorus—Oh! that beautiful home—oh! that beautiful world.

The ransomed throng, the sea of bliss,
The holy city of gorgeousness,
The verdant earth, the angel choir,
The flowers that never winter wear,
The conqueror's song, it sounds afar,
'Tis wafted on ambrosial air
Through endless years, we then shall prove,
The depths of a Savior's matchless love.

Chorus.

Printed at the Office of the "Reporter," Brodhead, Wis.

Truth customarily began her lectures with a favorite song or hymn. Her eloquence inspired some members of her audiences to dedicate poems to her.

region being turned into a free state, Congress passed stronger amendments to the Fugitive Slave Law, a strict measure that required the northern states to return runaway slaves to their masters.

The Fugitive Slave Law aroused greater sympathy for the abolitionist cause in the North. Many people echoed the feelings of the poet Ralph Waldo Emerson, who said, "This filthy enactment . . . I will not obey it, by God." Incensed by the harshness of the new law, antislavery sympathizers expanded the underground railroad network, which helped more than a thousand slaves escape from the

South each year. In some northern communities, slave catchers encountered armed resistance when confronting fugitive slaves and their supporters.

However, not all of the Northerners supported the abolitionists. Many Northerners believed that Fugitive Slave Law had to be obeyed in order to maintain peace between the North and the South, and they accused the abolitionists of trying to divide the nation. In addition, some groups in the North hated blacks and wanted all former slaves either returned to the South or deported to Africa.

During this divisive time for Americans, Truth's audiences were sometimes hostile to her cause. At times, she was even threatened by angry mobs. During these occasions, it took all of her courage to stand her ground on the podium.

In the midst of this turmoil in 1850, Truth joined an anti-slavery group led by the British abolitionist George Thompson. After spending a while with the group on a tour through eastern New York, she decided to continue westward by herself. She eventually arrived in Rochester, New York, the town where Frederick Douglass published his anti-slavery journal, *The North Star.* Truth gave many lectures during her extended stay in Rochester,

In the early 1850s, Truth became a household name throughout the United States. Eventually, posters were printed to announce her upcoming lectures.

FREE LECTURE!

SOJOURNER TRUTH,

Who has been a slave in the State of New York, and who has been a Lecturer for the last twenty-three years, whose character has been so vividly portrayed by Mrs. Harriet Breecher Stowe, as the African Sybil, will deliver a lecture upon the present issues of the day.

At   On

And will give her experiences as a Slave mother and religious woman. She comes highly recommended as a public speaker, having the approval of many thousands who have heard her earnest appeals, among whom are Wendell Phillips, Wm. Lloyd Garrison, and other distinguished men of the nation.

☞ At the close of her discourse she will offer for sale her photograph and a few of her choice songs.

whose residents were known for their strong abolitionist sympathies.

In May 1852, Truth left Rochester to attend a woman's rights convention in Akron, Ohio. While she was there, she made such a powerful defense of the feminist cause that it aroused national attention. The uneducated former slave who spoke in broken English was beginning to be recognized as one of the country's most talented public speakers. Many people admired her common sense approach to the issue of human rights and also enjoyed the humorous anecdotes that she used to support her arguments.

During the rest of 1852 and 1853, Truth continued her lecture tour in Ohio and Michigan. Friends lent her a horse and buggy for her travels, and a women's abolitionist group made her a white satin banner on which was embroidered the message: "Proclaim liberty throughout all the land and to all the inhabitants thereof." In every town that she visited, she attracted a crowd. Setting her banner on a pole in the ground, she would sing her favorite hymns until a crowd had gathered around her. Then she would begin her lecture. Even people who did not care deeply about the issue of slavery came to hear her speak.

In her travels through the Midwest, Truth was often heckled by proslavery groups. She relied on her quick wit to silence her critics. At one meeting, a man told her, "Old woman, I don't care any more for your talk than I do for the bite of a flea." The Lord willing," she replied, "I'll keep you scratching."

Truth also used anecdotes to explain her dissatisfaction with the Constitution, which she believed was badly flawed because it did not contain any laws protecting the liberties and rights of women and blacks. Speaking to a group of farmers whose wheat crops were being devastated by beetles, Truth told her audience how she had examined the grain and had found the weevils inside. She said:

> Now I hear talking about the Constitution and the rights of man. I come up and I take hold of this Constitution. It looks might big, and feel for my rights, but there aren't any ther. Then I say, "God, what ails this Constitution?" He says to me, "Sojourner, ther is a little weevil in it."

In mid-1853, after a successful tour through the Midwest, Truth decided to return east and visit members of her family. Her daughters were living in New York and New England; some had married and had children. Truth's oldest grandchild, Hannah's son James Caldwell, was already nine years old. After enjoying a pleasant stay with her daughter's families, Truth set out for her house in Northampton. But first she stopped in Andover, Massachusetts, the home of abolitionist writer Harriet Beecher Stowe.

The author of the immensely popular antislavery novel *Uncle Tom's Cabin,* Stowe had gained international renown after the book was published in 1852. Although her novel had aroused a furor among Southerners, who ac-

Harriet Beecher Stowe (left) helped win many adherents to the abolitionist cause with her novel Uncle Tom's Cabin. *She is shown her with her father, Lyman Beecher, and brother, Henry Ward Beecher, both of whom were ministers and active in the antislavery movement.*

cused her of greatly exaggerating the sufferings endured by slaves, abolitionists praised her for presenting a true picture of the injustices of the slave system, and her book helped to fan the antislavery fires in the North. The meeting between the tall black preacher and the diminutive white novelist proved to be memorable for both women.

After Truth returned home, she continued with her speaking tours. Whenever she attended an abolitionist or women's rights meeting, she always brought along several copies of her autobiography to sell as well as a new item: postcards that bore her photograph and the

To raise funds for her lecturing work, Truth sold postcards bearing her picture and personal motto. She referred to these cards as her cartes de visite.

Poet Frances E. W. Harper was a popular speaker on the abolitionist lecture circuit. Calling slavery "the giant sin of our country," she arroused support for the crusade against slavery with poems such as "The Slave Mother" and "Bury Me in a Free Land."

legend "I Sell the Shadow to Support the Substance." She called these cards her *cartes de visite,* which is French for "calling cards." She also brought her "Book of Life," an album in which she collected short notes and autographs from many of the people whom she had meet.

By the mid-1850s, the name of Sojourner Truth had become known throughout much of

America. However, she was not the only black woman whose anti-slavery efforts drew attention. During this period, the poet Frances E. W. Harper and the abolitionist Sarah Remond often addressed women's rights and anti-slavery conventions. Among the other black women who became noted as dedicated workers for black rights was Harriet Tubman, who led more than 300 slaves to freedom via the underground railroad.

As Truth continued to speak out for black emancipation, she insisted that freedom for blacks must be accompanied by freedom for women. "If colored men get their rights, and not colored women," she explained to the audience at a women's rights conference, "colored men will be masters over the women, and it will be just as bad as before."

As the women's rights movement grew, some of the feminists attempted to attract attention to their movement by adopting a style of dress known as "bloomers," which consisted of a jacket, a knee-length skirt, and baggy pants. This costume was very different from the awkward, hooped dresses that women usually wore. The opponents of women's rights soon began using the word "bloomers" as a term of ridicule for all feminists, but the less-constraining pants outfit became a symbol of

Featuring knee-length pants and baggy-sleeved jackets, the daring bloomers costume was favored by many feminists during Truth's time. A late 19th-century version of the outfit is shown here.

revolt to the women activists.

Truth disliked bloomers, which reminded her somewhat of the clothes that she had worn as a slave. (During those hateful times, she had been given a small strip of cloth to wear as a skirt, and because she was so tall, she had been forced to sew up the skirt between the legs for modesty's sake.) Instead, she continued to wear a plain dress and a shawl, preferring to indicate her dedication to the feminist movement in other ways.

During a women's rights convention in New York, Truth was jeered by an especially hostile group of men whenever she spoke. She told them that she knew how much it annoyed them to have a black woman speak to them about freedom and justice. Blacks and women, she stated, "have all been thrown down so low that nobody thought we'd ever get up again . . . but we will come up again, and now here I am."

This kind of uncompromising attitude eventually enabled Truth and other feminists to bring about some reforms. In New York, for example, Susan B. Anthony collected 10,000 signatures for a petition requesting that married women be allowed to control their own property. The state legislature ultimately approved Anthony's petition and also gave divorced women the right to share custody of their children.

As important as the issue of women's rights was during the 1850s, no issue resulted in greater public attention than the conflict between the North and South over the spread of slavery. In 1854, Illinois senator Stephen Douglas helped to win congressional approval for a plan that allowed settlers in Kansas and Nebraska to choose whether or not their territories would allow slavery. Guerrilla warfare

Democratic senator Sephen Douglas tried vainly to unite the North and South behind his plan for letting the residents of the western territories decide whether or not they wanted slavery. In 1858, he participated in a series of debates with one of America's most outspoken foes of slavery, Republican congressman Abraham Lincoln.

broke out between proslavery and anti-slavery groups in the two territories, and armed bands loyal to either side flooded in from other states. The most famous of the groups was led by the abolitionist John Brown.

The passage of Douglas's Kansas-Nebraska Act convinced many people in the North that Southerners would try to establish slavery throughout the West. Consequently, anti-slavery groups joined together in 1854 to form a new political party, the Republican party. Within a short time, the Republicans were challenging the powerful Democrats for control in the North, and the split between the two sections of the county, the North and the South, grew even wider.

In 1857, Truth decided to move to Battle Creek, Michigan. A town with strong abolitionist roots, it had proven to be a welcome stop for the 60 year old on several previous occasions. She settled in a local religious community called Harmonia and immediately attracted a group of friends and admirers.

However, Truth had only a brief time to enjoy the tranquility of her new home. In 1857, the Supreme Court stunned the North by ruling that Congress did not have the right to pass laws that restricted slavery. This new judicial ruling, which was called the Dred Scott decision (after a slave who had unsuccessfully petitioned the courts for his freedom), infuriated Northerners. They believed that the southern states would try to institute slavery throughout the country.

Shortly after the Dred Scott decision was announced, Truth returned to the anti-slavery lecture circuit and toured throughout Indiana, Illinois, and Iowa. Although many people listened to her warnings about the evils of slavery, others continued to jeer at her. One man even criticized her habit of smoking a pipe. Suggesting that a smoker's breath was not clean, he pointed out to her, "The Bible

An embattled John Brown holds one of his mortally wounded sons during his unsuccessful attempt to start a slave rebellion at Harper's Ferry, Virginia. Captured and hanged for treason, he was honored as a martyr by abolitionists.

tells us that no unclean thing can enter the kingdom of Heaven." That might be so, Truth admitted, "but when I go to Heaven I expect to leave my breath behind me."

By the end of the 1850s, the gulf between the North and the South had grown still wider, and the country seemed ready to split apart. Many black Americans doubted that slavery could ever be ended except through a violent overthrow of the state governments in the South. In 1859, John Brown's attempt to organize a slave rebellion at Harper's Ferry, Virginia, was crushed, turning him into a martyr for the abolitionist cause.

Truth was among the people who believed that slavery could still be ended peacefully. Years before, at an abolitionist meeting in Boston, Massachusetts, she and Frederick Douglass had tangled over this very issue. She had been sitting in the audience as Douglass gave a cheerless address about the prospects for slave emancipation. He had argued that only armed rebellion could free the slaves in the South, stating, "Slavery must end in blood."

At that point, Truth had interrupted his speech. "Frederick, is God dead?" she had asked him, implying there was hope that slavery would be eliminated without any bloodshed. It was a message that had heartened the audience.

Yet as the 1860s begin, it seemed increasingly likely that the battle over slavery would end in a bloodbath, as Douglass had predicted.

Chapter Seven

A
House
Divided

T HE NATION DEBATE over slavery reached the boiling point during the presidential campaign of 1860. Former Illinois congressman Abraham Lincoln, the Republican candidate for president, had earlier declared, "A house divided against itself cannot stand. . . . I believed this Government cannot endure permanently half slave and half free." Fiercely defending its right to treat people as property, the South threatened to establish its own separate slaveholding nation if Lincoln became president.

Lincoln's victory in the November elections

Children sit on the porch of a ruined mansion in Charleston, South Carolina, in April 1865. During the Civil War, huge areas of the South were devastated.

sparked a wide-scale rebellion in the South. By February 1861, seven states had seceded from the Union and formed their own confederate government. Four of the other eight slave states soon joined the Confederacy, and the North and the South prepared for war. The Civil War broke out on April 12, 1861, when Confederate units attacked the Union troops stationed at Fort Sumter, in Charleston, South Carolina.

Blacks and the anti-slavery societies hailed the war as a struggle to end slavery, but many Americans viewed it chiefly as a battle to reunite the country. Early in the war, the Union armies suffered a string of defeats, and hostility about being in a war was high in many areas of the North. Sojourner Truth decided to make a tour of the Midwest and rouse support for the Union's war effort.

During her tour, Truth was greeted by angry mobs in some places and by bands of supporters in others. Antiwar and antiblack feelings were especially high in Indiana, where the state legislature had passed a law forbidding blacks from entering the state. Truth defied the law and campaigned throughout the state for the Union cause. Arrested on numerous occasions, she was released each time when friendly crowds gathered to defend her with

In 1862, Truth traveled throughout the Midwest and spoke out in support of the Union cause. When an antiwar group in one town threatened to burn down the lecture hall in which Truth was scheduled to speak, she vowed, "Then I will speak upon its ashes."

shouts of "Sojourner, Free Speech, and the Union."

Exhausted by the rigors of her tour, Truth returned home to recuperate. In 1860, her daughter Elizabeth and two of her grandsons had moved to Battle Creek. A little later, her daughter Diana joined them. Having her family nearby not only gave Truth great comfort but also reminded her that all of her children had been released from slavery.

Despite this feeling of comfort, Truth still had to find the means to support herself. More than 60 years old and no longer able to perform strenuous work, she cooked and did cleaning chores for people in Battle Creek and

went to abolitionist conventions with armfuls
of her book to sell. All of this activity weakened her.

During the Civil War, great numbers of escaped slaves fled to Union army camps. Many of the runaways served the Northern troops as cooks, wagon drivers, construction workers, and spies.

Truth's strength was momentarily restored after President Lincoln signed the Emancipation Proclamation, which declared that all

slaves in the rebelious Confederate states
would be free on January 1, 1863. But Truth
soon became too ill to work or travel. Before
long, her family ran into financial difficulties.

Word of Truth's dire situation reached the
abolitionist newspaper *Anti-Slavery Standard,*
and its editors collected donations for her from
their readers. She was grateful for the much-
needed assistance, and she used the money to
buy a small house in Battle Creek. A friend
of hers named Frances Titus, who arranged
for the publication of a new, revised edition of
The Narrative of Sojourner Truth, also

Abraham Lincoln (in top hat) meets with officers who commanded the Union troops at the Battle of Antietam, in September 1862. Shortly afterward, the president issued the Emanicipation Proclamation, which granted freedom to slaves in Confederate states.

answered Truth's mail for her and later became the manager of her lecture tours.

Truth's fame increased after Harriet Beecher Stowe wrote an account of her 1853 meeting with Truth and published it in the April 1863 issue of the *Atlantic* magazine. People who had never before heard of Truth were introduced to the amazing exploits of the woman whom Stowe called the "African Sibyl," a reference to a prophetess of ancient times. Stowe marveled over Truth's great intellectual abilities and wondered what other feats this illiterate former slave would have ac-

On October 29, 1864, Truth met Lincoln in the president's office in the White House to give him some moral support. This painting shows the president examining her "Book of Life."

complished had she learned how read and write.

Although Truth was illiterate, she lacked nothing in either eloquence or vision. She only wished that she was younger so that she could help lead blacks in their struggle for freedom. Now was the time for black men to take up arms to save the nation, she said, for the sins of the white men had been so great "that they don't know God, nor God don't know them."

In the beginning of the Civil War, blacks had not been accepted as soldiers in the Union army. However, after the Emancipation Proclamation was issued, the North began to recruit blacks to serve in racially segregated regiments. Although black soldiers received poor pay and were sometimes mistreated by their white officers, many men enlisted in the black regiments and fought gallantly for the cause of freedom.

In November 1863, Truth traveled to Camp Ward, an army base near Detroil, Michigan, where 1,500 black troops were stationed. She brought food donated by the residents of Battle Creek so that the soldiers could enjoy a proper Thanksgiving dinner. Upon her arrival, the regiment's commanding officer ordered to stand at attention. Truth then spoke to them about patriotism, and when she finished, the soldiers gave her a rousing cheer. She remained after the official ceremony to help prepare the Thanksgiving meal, and while the men ate, she sang hymns for them.

In the spring of 1864, still just recently recovered from her long illness, Truth decided to visit President Lincoln in Washington, D.C. Although many of her abolitionist friends believed that Lincoln was moving too slowly in bringing about an end to slavery, she greatly respected the president. "Have patience!" she told them. "It takes a great while to turn about this great ship of state." In the meantime, she thought that Lincoln could use some encouragement.

Truth did not tell anyone about her travel plan until the day of her departure, when she was working as a laundress for a Battle Creek family. "I've got to hurry with this washing," she told her employers. When they asked her why she was so pressed for time, she replied, "Because I'm leaving for Washington this afternoon. I'm going down there to advise the president."

Accompanied by her grandson Sam Banks, Truth boarded a train for the nation's capital, stopping in several towns along the way to give speeches. She reached Washington, D.C., in

September 1864, a little more than a month
before Americans were to go to the polls and
decide whether Lincoln should be given a second term in office. The president faced strong
opposition from the Copperheads, the antiwar
faction of the Democratic party, who wanted

After Union armies liberated large sections of the South, thousands of freed slaves began to move north and settle in refugee camps around Washington, D.C.

to sign an immediate peace with the South and leave slavery intact.

On the morning of October 29, 1864, Truth joined a group of people waiting in the White House's reception room for their appointment with the president. An abolitionist friend had

The newly freed slaves who flooded into Washington's refugee set-tlements suffered from poverty, disease, and starvation. In 1865, Con-gress established the Freedmen's Bureau, whose agencies provided blacks with food and surplus clothing.

made the arrangements for Truth to meet with Lincoln. When the president appeared from time to time to usher someone into his officer, she was pleased to see that he treated his black guests with the same courtesy that he show-ed to his white visitors.

Finally, Truth was invited into the presi-dent's office. She made a long examination of the tall, thin president noted that the stresses he had endured while leading his country had left him looking extremely weary. After sitting down, she bluntly told him, "I never heard of you before you were put in for president." Lincoln laughed before replying, "I heard of you years and years before I ever thought of being president."

Truth then thanked the president for all he had done for black Americans and advised him not to worry about the blustering attacks of his critics. The people were behind him and would support him in the upcoming election, she said. Lincoln in turn thanked her for the encouragement and then signed her "Book of Life." He wrote, "For Aunty Sojourner Truth, A. Lincoln, Oct. 29, 1864."

In November, Lincoln was swept back into office by an overwhelming margin in the wake of several victories by the Union army. By that time, Truth had discovered that she greatly enjoyed the busy atmosphere in the capital. Instead of returning to Battle Creeek, she decided to remain in Washington, D.C., and see what she could do to assist the Union's war effort.

At the request of Henry Highland Garnet, a prominent black minister, Truth spoke at a local charity benefit to help raise money for black soldiers. She also joined a group of women who were feeding and nursing

During the Civil War, hotels such as this one in Washington, D.C., were turned into medical buildings to care for the huge numbers of wounded soldiers. Near the end of the war, Truth worked at a hospital run by the Freedmen's Bureau.

thousands of former slaves who had fled to the North. The trickle of fugitives escaping from southern plantations steadily increased as the war progressed and the Union armies captured ever larger sections of the Confederacy. Many of the escaped slaves settled in the nation's capital, which had become a free area in April 1862 after Lincoln signed a bill outlawing slavery there.

The recently freed slaves endured abominable conditions in the nation's capital. They lived in temporary refugee camps (known as freedmen's villages) which had been set up by charity organizations and government agencies. The camps were little more than clusters of shacks. To stay warm in the winter, the men and women covered themselves with rags, and they ate scraps gleaned from garbage dumps to keep from starving. Many became sick and died.

In addition to the freedmen's other adversities, they also had to hide from a bands of slave traders who kidnapped blacks and smuggled them into Confederate states. The kidnappers threatened to kill anyone who gave information about the illegal slave trade to federal marshals. Most freedmen were afraid to speak out in protest.

However, Truth refused to be silenced. She marched through the freedmen's villages and told the slaves, "The law is for you. Take refuge in it." When policemen who had been bribed by the slave traders told Truth that they would arrest her if she continued to cause trouble, she said, "If you put me in the guard house, I will shake the United States rock like a cradle."

Truth's attacks on racial injustice in the nation's capital boosted the morale of the black community. Toward the end of 1864, a public welfare organization called the National Freedman's Relief Association asked her to

As Northerners prepared to celebrate the Union victory in the Civil War, they learned the tragic news that Lincoln had died after being shot by a Confederate sympathizer named John Wilkes Booth.

work as a counselor to former slaves who were living in a camp in Arlington Heights, Virginia. There she educated the freedmen about the need to find work and housing and about other responsibilities that came with their newly won freedom.

In 1865, the Freedmen's Bureau, a federal relief agency, appointed Truth to an administrative position in the Freedmen's Hospital in Washington, D.C. She did her best to ensure that proper medical care was given to the hospital's black patients, who became used to hearing her tell them, "Be clean, Be clean." The work gave her a renewed sense of purpose, and she began to feel stronger than she had in some time.

Truth was still in Washington, D.C., on the night of April 14, 1865, when Lincoln was assassinated while watching the performance of a play at Ford's Theater. He died the following morning. Truth, who believed that no one had done more for the cause of black Americans than Lincoln, was among those who were devastated by his passing.

In the month following Lincoln's death, the last of the Confederate armies surrendered to Union forces. The Civil War had spanned four years and had taken hundreds of thousands of lives. But the battle against slavery—abetted by black soldiers, who had composed nearly 10 percent of the North's troops by the end of the war—had been won. Truth's prayers had been answered; she had lived to see the end of slavery.

On December 12, 1865, Truth and millions of other Americans celebrated as Congress ratified the Thirteenth Amendment to the U.S. Constitution. This amendment declared that "neither slavery nor involuntary servitude. . .shall exist within the United States or any place subject to their jurisdiction." A little more than two-and-a-half centuries after being established in America, slavery was at last officially abolished.

Chapter Eight

"I Want to Ride!"

FROM THE SOUTH, long dark shadows of dissent stretched over the blood-soaked earth, threatening to engulf the bright promise of the freedoms that had been won during the Civil War. The passions that had ignited and fueled the war still raged in the hearts of many Americans as millions of former slaves celebrated their liberation. While Sojourner Truth looked forward to the period ahead as a time of great opportunity, when the country would throw off the chains of oppression and bigotry that had confined blacks, she realized that a strong core of racial

The decade following the Civil War was a period of progress for civil rights legislation. During the late 1860s, black male citizens began to vote in large numbers for the first time.

Blacks who served in Congress shortly after the Civil War included (first row, from left) Hiram Revels, Benjamin Turner, Josiah Walls, Joseph Rainey, and Robert Elliot; (second row, from left) Robert DeLarge and Jefferson Long.

hatred remained within the United States and that it would take a long struggle to overcome the prejudices that had formed through the centuries.

Choosing to stay in Washington, D.C., Truth prepared herself for a new campaign against racism. The slaves had been freed, but in the eyes of many whites throughout the country, blacks were not yet equal. Opponents of racial equality began to press for new measures that would deprive blacks fo the rights enjoyed by other American citizens. In the South, state legislatures composed of ex-Confederates passed laws known as the Black Codes, which were designed to keep freedmen in a state of servitude.

Even in the nation's capital, examples of racial prejudice were starkly evident. In one case, blacks were forced to ride in the less comfortable sections of streetcars or in separate vehicles altogether. Truth organized a protest against the streetcar company, and the firm's president agreed to issue new rules forbidding segregated seating.

However, not everyone accepted the new rules. One day, Truth tried to flag down a streetcar, but the conductor refused to stop for her. After a while, she saw another streetcar approaching. Stepping in front of it, she yelled, "I want to ride! I want to ride!" Curious people gathered around her and blocked the streetcar's way. She quickly boarded the car and sat down in the section that had once been reserved for whites.

The conductor was enraged by Truth's actions and ordered her to sit in another section or to get off the car. She calmly replied that she would sit wherever she wished. After a while, the conductor permitted the car to continue on, with Truth still in her seat. "Bless God! I have had a ride!" she said, summing up not only her latest encounter but her entire life.

Another incident occurred when Truth boarded a streetcar with a white friend named Laura Haviland. The conductor pushed Truth aside and said, "Get out of the way and let this lady come in."

"I am a lady too," Truth said to him before climbing on board.

As the two women continued on their way, a white man asked the conductor if blacks were allowed on the streetcar. In response to the man's question, the conductor took hold of Truth's shoulder and ordered her to get off, but she refused. Haviland then took her friend's arm and told the man to leave them alone. When the conductor asked Haviland if Truth was a servant who belonged to her, Haviland answered, "no, she belongs to humanity."

Yet this answer still did not leave the conductor satisfied. He shoved Truth, and she dislocated her shoulder. She later sued him for assault and battery and not only won her case but succeeded in having him removed from his job.

Even with these incidents, Truth's thoughts were less on her own troubles than on the suffering of others. It especially saddened her to

Truth protested aganst discriminatory laws that denied the ballot to women and—in some areas—blacks and illiterate citizens. After she was once turned away from a voting booth, she said, "I can't read a book, but I can read the people."

see the contrast between the resplendent buildings occupied by federal agencies and the slums in which the newly freed blacks were forced to live. It seemed unjust to her that

blacks should live in such squalor after all they
had done to build the country. "We have been
a source of wealth to this republic," she maintained. "Our nerves and sinews, our tears and
blood, have been sacrificed...our unpaid labor
has been a stepping-stone to its financial success. Some of its dividends must surely be
ours."

During the period following the Civil War,
some attempts were made to help the South's
former slaves adjust to their new status as free
American citizens. Congress passed the Civil

Although Truth applauded the efforts of federal agencies to set up schools for blacks in the South, she believed that the government should be doing more to help black farmers become independent of white landowners. In 1868, she began a campaign to help former slaves obtain free land in the western territories.

Rights Act, which nullified the Southern states' Black Codes. The Freedmen's Bureau helped to feed and provide shelter for former slaves and established many school for blacks. Despite these measures, most blacks continued to live in desperate poverty and were still being victimized by racial prejudice.

One of the ways to help out blacks, Truth realized, was by making beneficial use of the land out west, in California, Oregon, the Dakota territory, Nebraska, and Kansas. The federal government had already granted huge tracts of land to railroad companies in an attempt to encourage the construction of a transcontinental railway. Some of that land, Truth insisted, must be given to black Americans, whom she believed to be well deserving.

In 1868, Truth began her campaign to persuade Congress to grant land in the West to black settlers. She met with a group of senators who told her that she needed to present them with a petition and thousands of letters in support of her proposal. Senator Charles Sumner, a longtime abolitionist leader, advised her to go on a speaking tour and get the support of the people.

Although Truth was now in her 70s, she once again took to the road to fight for a cause in which she believed. She traveled throughout the East and Midwest and spoke out against the unjust way in which blacks were being treated. As she lectured, she called upon her audiences to sign her land-grant petition so that she could bring "tons of paper down to Washington for those spouters [congressmen] to chew on."

As Truth carried out her mission, the routine must have seemed very familiar. She often spoke to friends about how much she still had to do, how many miles she still had to cover.

Much of the post-Civil War progress in black rights occurred during the presidency of Ulysses S. Grant. In 1870, Truth met the former Union commanding general at the White House.

At an age when most people were sedentary, she was not yet ready to rest.

While Truth was conducting her tour through the North, the South was undergoing the process called Reconstruction. During this period, the former rebel states were forced to alter their racist laws before being readmitted to the Union. In addition to these changes, new laws passed by Congress in the late 1860s gave blacks further hope that America was at last willing to grant them equality. In 1868, Congress ratified the Four-

White supremacists such as the two Ku Klux Klan members shown here used terror and violence against southern blacks in their efforts to overturn the new civil rights law passed by Congress.

teenth Amendment of the Constitution, which granted American citizenship to all blacks and allegedly gave them full civil rights. Congress also passed a number of laws providing federal protection for southern freedmen.

Truth often returned to Washington, D.C., in the middle of her travels. On March 31, 1870, she went with several other people to the White House to meet with Ulysses S. Grant, the former commander of the Union armies who had been elected president in 1868. As the meeting began, both Truth and Grant were stiff and very formal with one another.

But by the end of the meeting, when Truth, her eyes glowing with emotion, thanked Grant for his efforts to secure new guarantees of justice for blacks, the president was moved. He replied that he hoped to be wise and firm, and to remember that everyone deserved full rights. Then he signed Truth's "Book of Life" and took one of her calling cards as a memento of their meeting.

The meeting caped off a memorable pair of days for Truth. On the previous day, Congress had ratified the Fifteenth Amendment, guaranteeing the right to vote to all men regardless of "race, color, or previous condition of servitude." The right to vote was crucial to the welfare of blacks, who made up a sizable portion of the southern population and composed the majority in some states.

Before long, black voters began to make their numbers felt and increased their representation in state legislatures. In addition, more than 20 black leaders—including Blanche K. Bruce, P.B.S. Pinchback, Joseph Rainey, and Hiram Revels—were elected to Congress during the Reconstruction era. The work of these legislators helped to end more than 200 years of enforced ignorance as blacks throughout the South began to attend free schools and acquire the knowledge that could

help them succeed in a free society.

While Truth applauded the progress that blacks were making in the South, she was still concerned about the impoverished freedmen who had flocked to Washington, D.C. She remained convinced that their only opportunity for a rewarding life lay in the western territories, where they might be able to live free of the prejudice that they faced in both the South and the East. In 1871, she implored a white audience in Rochester, New York, to sign her petition and help the former slaves resettle in the West. "You owe it to them," she said, "because you took away from them all they earned."

Although Truth amassed many signatures for the land-grant petition, her plan found lit-

A former teacher at a black school in the South tells a Senate committee about how he was beaten by Ku Klux Klan members.

tle support in Washington, D.C., and was never adopted. The tide of black progress continued to be blocked by conservative whites. More and more, Truth began to realize that the battle for black freedom had only begun.

In the South, many whites rebelled against the Reconstruction laws and formed white-supremacist groups such as the Ku Klux Klan, which kidnapped and murdered blacks without fear of punishment. White insurrectionists conspired to overthrow the southern state governments in which blacks had succeeded in marshalling a great deal of power. Blacks armed themselves and fought back, and Grant was forced to send regiments of federal troops to South Carolina and other troubled areas to restore order.

Truth was sustained by a large group of friends and relatives during her final years in Battle Creek, Michigan. Her daughter Diana Corbin (shown here) was among those who attended her.

The Supreme Court supported the anti-Reconstruction forces by issuing rulings that weakened the effects of the Fourteenth and Fifteenth Amendments. The Justices ruled that the federal government had only limited power to protect southern black voters. It seems that by July 4, 1876—the centenary of the signing of the Declaration of Independence—white Americans had still not decided if they really believed that "all Men are created equal." However, by the end of the year, they had in effect decided—and Truth cannot have liked their decision.

The initial results of the 1876 presidential election indicated that the victor was the Democratic candidate, Samuel Tilden, by a narrow margin. However, Republicans bribed the electoral officers of Louisiana and Florida to change their voting tallies and thus switch their states' electoral votes to the Republican candidate, Rutherford Hayes. These Republicans promised that the new administration would let conservative whites regain control of the South.

With a change in the electoral vote, Hayes (and not Tilden) became the 19th president of the United States. One of his first major acts as president was to withdraw the federal troops that were helping to protect the civil rights of southern blacks. The action signaled that the Reconstruction era was over and the gains that blacks had won after the Civil War would now be rolled back. Despite the significance of this action, Truth did not have the strength to go on a speaking tour and protest against the new attempts to deprive blacks of their rights.

Rumors began to circulate that Truth had died, or that she was too old to travel, having already celebrated her 100th birthday. She was actually nearly 80 years old and living at her home in Battle Creek. Although her hair had turned gray 30 years before, by now her hearing and sight had almost disappeared. To walk, she needed the support of a cane.

In 1877, according to some accounts, Truth's health mysteriously improved. Perhaps her spirit was strengthened by the knowledge that wherever there was oppression, courageous people like herself were rising up to carry on the battle for freedom. In any case, her hearing returned and her eyesight sharpened dramatically. She told her friend Olive Gilbert that the Lord had "put new glasses in the window of her soul." A newspaper reporter who visisted her at this time wrote that her gray hair had turned black again and that her skin was almost free of wrinkles. "It is the mind that makes the body," Truth maintained.

Yet by the beginning of 1882, Truth had become gravely ill. Painful ulcers began to cover her arms and legs, and she became too weak to get up from bed. She remained this way for the next year and a half. According

"The Spirit calls me, I must go," said Truth on the day that she started her journey as God's pilgrim. Fortified by her immense courage and deep spiritual faith, she devoted her life to the cause of freedom and equality for all people.

to Olive Gilbert, "Her life's forces were spent."

One morning in early November 1883, Gilbert visited Truth and found her in extreme pain. Yet when Truth saw her old friend, she smiled, and with a faraway look in her eyes, she began to sing her favorite hymn, which she had often used to gather crowds for her speeches. She sang:

It was early in the morning,
It was early in the morning,
Just at the break of day,
When He rose, when he rose, when He rose,
And went to heaven on a cloud.

Two weeks later, at her home in Battle Creek, Truth sank into a deep coma. She died early in the morning of November 26, 1883, at the age of about 86. She did not fear death, she had said, for she was confident that she would be happy in heaven.

Two days after Truth's death, nearly a thousand people gathered at her house and formed a procession behind the black-plumed hearse that bore her body. Her coffin was decorated with the images of a cross, a sheaf of ripe grain, a sickle, and a crown. A service was held for her in a nearby church, and many of her fellow activists in the women's rights and abolitionist movements spoke about her "rare qualities of head and heart."

The sun was setting just as Truth was lowered into her final resting place. A crimson and gold sky kit up the western horizon. Gilbert later said that the sun seemed "unwilling to leave the earth in gloom."

When the sun finally set, millions of stars lit up the heavens in which Truth had found assurance that God was watching over her.

In return for God's guidance, Truth became His faithful servant, continually ignoring personal hardship in her pursuit of freedom for women and blacks. "I think of the great things of God," she said, "not the little things." Deeply devoted to turning the world "right side up," she traveled far and wide to leave an inspiring legacy to all those who face a long and difficult journey when fighting for justice and respect.

CHRONOLOGY

1797	Born Isabella in Hurley, New York
1800	Master, Johannes Hardenbergh, dies; Isabella becomes the property of Charles Hardenbergh
1808	Sold to John Nearly
1809	Sold to Martin Schryver; Isabella's mother and father die
1810	Sold to John Dumont
1814	Marries Thomas, a fellow slave
1826	Sold to Isaac Van Wagener
1827	Officially freed from slavery
1828	Moves to New York City
1832	Joins the Zion Hill commune
1843	Changes name to Sojourner Truth
1844	Joins the Northampton Association of Education and Industry in Massachusetts
1850	Publishes *The Narrative of Sojourner Truth*
1857	Moves to Battle Creek, Michigan
1864	Meets with President Abraham Lincoln; joins the National Freedmen's Relief Association
1865	Works in the Freedmen's Hospital
1870	Meets with President Ulysses S. Grant
1883	Dies in Battle Creek, Michigan on Nov. 26

FURTHER READING

Bernard, Jacqueline. *Journey Toward Freedom*. New York: Norton, 1967.

Corbin, Carole L. *The Right to Vote*. New York: Franklin Watts, 1985.

Dunster, Mark. *Sojourner Truth*. Fresno, CA: Linden Publications, 1983.

Fauset, Arthur Hill. *Sojourner Truth: God's Faithful Pilgrim*. Chapel Hill: University of North Carolina Press, 1938.

Gilbert, Olive. *Narrative of Sojourner Truth*. New York: Arno Press, 1968.

Hooks, Bell. *Ain't I a Woman: Black Women and Feminism*. Boston: South End Press, 1981.

McManus, Edgar J. *A History of Negro Slavery in New York*. Syracuse, NY: Syracuse University Press, 1966.

Ortiz, Victoria. *Sojourner Truth, A Self-Made Woman*. New York: Lippincott, 1974.

Pauli, Hertha. *Her Name Was Sojourner Truth*. New York: Appleton-Century Crofts, 1962.

Pinney, Roy. *Slavery—Past and Present*. New York: Thomas Nelson, 1972.

Porter, Kirk H. *A History of Suffrage in the United States*. New York: AMS Press, 1971.

INDEX

Abolition movement,
10-11, 14, 19, 94-103,
109-123, 129, 133, 141,
149
Akron, Ohio, 9, 15, 116
Albany, New York, 77
American and Foreign
Anti-Slavery Society,
104
American Anti-Slavery
Society, 96, 102
Andover, Massachusetts,
118
Anthony, Susan B., 100,
125
Anti-Slavery Standard 136
Arlington Heights,
Virginia, 147
Atlantic, 137

Banks, Sam (grandson),
141
Battle Creek Michigan,
127, 132, 145, 166-169
Benson, George, 94-95
Bible, 18, 76, 89-90, 124
Black codes, 153, 156
Black troops, 140-141
Bloomers, 123-124
Boston, Massachusetts,
129
Brooklyn New York, 88
Brown, John, 126-129
Brown, William Wells, 97

Bruce, Blanche K., 161

Caldwell, James (grand-
son), 118
California, 112
Camp Ward, Michigan,
140
Canada, 100
Catlin, Robert, 42-47
Civil Rights Act, 156
Civil War, 138, 140, 142,
145-149, 156, 165
Compromise of 1850, 103
Congress U.S., 112, 149,
158, 161
Constitution, U.S., 67,
117, 149, 159, 161,
164-165
Copperheads, 142

Declaration of In-
dependence, 104, 165
Declaration of Sentiments
and Resolutions, 104
Democratic party, 126,
142, 165
Detroit Michigan, 140
Douglas Stephen, 125
Douglass, Frederick, 12,
94-97, 129-130
Dred Scott decision, 127
Dumont John, 41, 46-47,
49, 51-52, 55, 57, 58,
66-67, 85, 95

Dumont, Thomas (husband) 49-50, 53, 67

Elijah the Tishbite, *See* Pierson, Elijah
Emancipation, in New York State, 51, 59
Emancipation Proclamation, 135, 140
Emerson, Ralph Waldo, 114

Folser, Anne, 79
Folger, Benjamin, 78-79, 83
Fort Sumter, South Carolina, 132
Freedmen, 146, 148, 149, 152, 156-157
Freedmen's Bureau, 148, 156, 157
Freedmen's Hospital 148
Free Soil party, 96
Fugitive Slave Law, 114-115

Gage, Frances, 11, 15, 17
Garnet, Henry Highland, 145
Garrison, William Lloyd, 11, 94-96, 103, 109
Gedney, Solomon, 58-63
Gilbert, Olive, 97, 166-167
Grant, Ulysses S., 160
Grimke, Angelina, 66, 100
Grimke, Sarah, 100

Hardenbergh, Betsey (mother), 23-24, 26-30, 35
Hardenbergh, Charles, 25, 35
Hardenbergh, Isabella. *See* Truth Sojourner
Hardenbergh, James (father), 23-24, 26, 35-38
Hardenbergh, Johannes, 23
Hardenbergh, Michael (brother), 31-34
Hardenbergh, Nancy (sister), 31
Hardenbergh, Peter (brother), 27, 28, 67-73
Harmonia, 127
Harper, Frances E. W., 123
Harper's Ferry, Virginia, 129
Haviland, Laura, 154
Hayes, Rutherford B., 165
Henson, Josiah, 97
Hill, Samuel, 94
Hurley, New York, 21

Ireland, 71

Kansas-Nebraska Act, 126
Kingdom, The. *See* Zion Hill
Kingston, New York, 35, 59, 60, 65
Ku Klux Klan, 163

Liberator, The, 94
Liberty party, 96
Lincoln, Abraham, 131-136, 141-146, 149
London England, 103
Long Island, New York, 89
Magdalen Asylum, 75-79

Matthews, Robert, 71-81, 91
Matthias, *See* Matthews, Robert
Mexico, 100
Michigan, 117
Mormons, 76
Mott, Lucretia, 14, 100-101, 103, 105

Narrative of Frederick Douglas, The, 97
Narrative of Sojourner Truth, The 13, 98, 136
National Freedman's Relief Association, 94
Nealy, John (owner), 35-38
New England Anti-Slavery Society, 94
New Netherlands, 23-25
New Paltz, New York, 41, 60, 65-67, 94
New York City, 68-73, 75, 80-83, 85
Northampton Society, 94
North Star, The, 115
Northup, Solomon, 97

Philips, Wendell, 109
Pierson, Elijah, 159-162
Pinchback, P. B. S., 161
Quakers, *See* Society of Friends

Rainsey, Joseph, 161
Reconstruction, 159-162, 163
Remond, Sarah, 123
Republican party, 126, 131, 165
Revels, Hiram, 161

Revival meetings, 77
Rochester, New York, 115, 162
Ruggles, David, 94

Schryver, Martin (owner) 37-38
Seneca Falls, New York, 164
Slave narratives, 96-97
Slave traders, 31-34, 84, 114
Society of Friends, 55, 59, 61, 65
Stanton, Elizabeth Cady, 14, 103, 105
Stone, Lucy, 100, 105
Stowe Harriet Beecher, 118-119, 137
Supreme Court, U.S., 164

Tappan, Lewis, 101
Thompson, George, 115
Tilden, Samuel, 163
Titus, Frances, 136-137
Truth, Sojourner
    in abolition movement 10-15
    as "African sibyl," 137
    appearance of 110-166
    autobiography of, 13, 91-98, 122
    "Book of Life," 122, 145, 161
    born, 23
    changes name, 23, 88-90
    childhood of, 25-38
    children of, 50-51, 64, 80, 118, 133
    efforts for land grand 158, 160

escape from slavery,
52-53
freed from slavery,
13-53
funeral of, 168-169
grandchildren of, 118,
136, 141
helps black troops,
140-141, 147, 157
helps ex-slaves, 145-149
illiteracy of, 13, 59-69,
90, 97, 137
last years and death,
166-169
lawsuits by, 59-63, 83,
154
as lecturer, 109-118,
133-137, 145, 157-159
life as slave, 13, 25-38,
41-42
marriage of, 49-51, 53,
67
meets President Grant,
160, 161
meets President Lin-
coln, 131-136
at Northampton
Associaiton, 94-95
parents of, 23-36, 38
as preacher, 84-85,
97-91
religion and, 25-28,
49-51, 55-56, 67-70,
74-85, 87-93, 166-169
sale of, 35-38, 41-42, 53
sale of family, 35
siblings of, 27-35
and women's rights,
9-21, 103-107, 115-123
Tubman, Harriet, 123
Uncle Tom's Cabin (Store),
118
Underground Railroad,
100, 114-115, 123
Ulster County, New York,
71

Vale, Gilbert, 83-84
Van Wagener, Isaac and
Maria, 55-58, 61, 65-70

Ward, Samuel Ringgold,
97
Washington, D.C.,
142-146, 149, 152-154,
160-163
Whiting family, 81-83, 88
Women's rights
arguments against,
14-21
conventions, 9-21,
103-107, 117, 125
movement, 14-15,
100-107, 109-111, 123,
124-125
Worcester, Massachusetts,
105
World Antislavery Con-
vention, 102

Zion Hill, 78-81, 91

PHOTO CREDITS

PETER KRASS has written for *Current Biography* and many other magazines, journals, and newspapers, as well as for an international news service, newsletters, radio broadcasts, and films. He was a Cine Golden Eagle Award-winner in 1986. He lives in Brooklyn, New York.

NATHAN IRVIN HUGGINS is W.E.B. Du Bois Professor of History and Director of the W.E.B. Du Bois Institute for Afro-American Research at Harvard University. He previously taught at Columbia University. Professor Huggins is the author of numerous books, including *Black Odyssey: The Afro-American Ordeal in Slavery, The Harlem Renaissance,* and *Slave and Citizen: The Life of Frederick Douglass.*

THE MELROSE SQUARE BLACK AMERICAN SERIES
PRESENTS
A NEW ILLUSTRATED BIOGRAPHY OF

Ida B. Wells
By Joe Nazel

With the end of Reconstruction, reactionary
whites in the South sought, through the cre-
ation of Jim Crow laws, to take away the rights
only recently won by African Americans. One
woman, a schoolteacher named Ida B. Wells,

stood up to fight for her
rights, refusing to leave a
first-class railway seat for
which she had paid. When
she sued the railroad and
took her case to the U S.
Supreme Court, she gained
the attention and respect of
black journalists. Soon she
herself began writing for
newspapers and fighting
not only the new concept of
segregation but also a rising tide of lynching that
was sweeping the nation. When her newspaper
office in Memphis was destroyed, she moved
north and helped found the NAACP and spent
most of the rest of her life in efforts to end injustice. Order your copy by sending $6.50 (includes
shipping and handling) to Melrose Square, 8060
Melrose, Los Angeles, California, 90046. California residents, please add $0.40 sales tax.

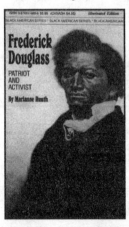

THE MELROSE SQUARE BLACK AMERICAN SERIES
PRESENTS
A NEW ILLUSTRATED BIOGRAPHY OF

NAT TURNER

By Terry Bisson

Born into slavery in 1800, Nat Turner held the strong
conviction that he was born to put an end to the institution of slave holding. His courage, to rise up against
a powerful system, is to this day an inspiration to those
who seek liberty and freedom. In the early morning
hours of August 22, 1831, Turner and his "chosen four"
in addition to two other slaves, slipped into the main
house of his legal master, Joseph Travis in Southamp-
tion County, Virginia. "General Nat" as he was named
by his loyal followers, knew
that it must be done. As the
rest of the country lay in
peace, Turner struck his
Master Travis with a blunt
sword and began a trail of
bloody death that set off a
powerful revolt. Order your
copy of this biography. Send
$5.50 (includes shipping
and handling) to Melrose
Square, 8060 Melrose
Avenue, Los Angeles, Cal-
ifornia, 90046. California
residents, please add $0.35
state tax.